320 SAT Math Subject Test Problems arranged by Topic and Difficulty Level

Level 2

A Proven Roadmap to
Your First-Choice College

Dr. Steve Warner

Table of Contents

ACTIONS TO COMPLETE BEFORE YOU READ THIS BOOK

1. Purchase a TI-84 or equivalent calculator

It is recommended that you use a TI-84 or comparable calculator for the SAT Math Subject Test. Answer explanations in this book will always assume you are using such a calculator.

2. Take a practice SAT from the Official Guide to get your preliminary SAT math score

Use this score to help you determine the problems you should be focusing on (see page 9 for details).

3. Claim your FREE book

Simply visit the following webpage and enter your email address to receive an electronic copy of *The 32 Most Effective SAT Math Strategies* for FREE:

www.thesatmathprep.com/320SATLvL2.html

4. 'Like' my Facebook page

This page is updated regularly with SAT prep advice, tips, tricks, strategies, and practice problems. Visit the following webpage and click the 'like' button.

www.facebook.com/SATPrepGet800

INTRODUCTION
THE PROPER WAY TO PREPARE

There are many ways that a student can prepare for the SAT Math Level 2 Subject Test. But not all preparation is created equal. I always teach my students the methods that will give them the maximum result with the minimum amount of effort.

The book you are now reading is self-contained. Each problem was carefully created to ensure that you are making the most effective use of your time while preparing for the test. By grouping the problems given here by level and topic I have ensured that you can focus on the types of problems that will be most effective to improving your score.

I recommend beginning SAT Math Subject Test preparation after you have prepared for the SAT Reasoning Test. All of the math preparation you have already completed will be useful when taking the Subject Test. In particular, all the strategies that I teach for the SAT Reasoning Test can be used for the Subject Test as well.

You may want to take the SAT Math Subject Test about one or two months after you have taken the SAT for the first time (assuming you have prepared effectively for it). Note that I recommend three to four months of preparation for the SAT. Only one or two additional months is required for the Subject Test because all of the preparation you have already done will still be useful.

If you have not yet decided if you will take the Level 1 or Level 2 test, I strongly recommend you take a College Board practice test of each one to determine which is best for you. Note that the curve on the Level 2 test is much stronger, so even if you feel like you are doing much worse on the Level 2 test, you may wind up with a higher score. If your Level 2 score is less than 50 points lower than your Level 1 score, you may want to go for the Level 2 test. If you use this book to prepare you should see a significant improvement in your score.

1. Using this book effectively
- Begin studying at least one month before test day
- Practice Math Subject Test problems twenty minutes each day
- Choose a consistent study time and location

You will retain much more of what you study if you study in short bursts rather than if you try to tackle everything at once. So try to choose about a twenty-minute block of time that you will dedicate to the SAT math subject test each day. Make it a habit. The results are well worth this small time commitment.

- Every time you get a question wrong, **mark it off, no matter what your mistake**.
- Begin each study session by first redoing problems from previous study sessions that you have marked off.
- If you get a problem wrong again, **keep it marked off**.

Note that this book often emphasizes solving each problem in more than one way. Please listen to this advice. The same question is not generally repeated on any SAT Subject Test so the important thing is learning as many techniques as possible.

Being able to solve any specific problem is of minimal importance. The more ways you have to solve a single problem the more prepared you will be to tackle a problem you have never seen before, and the quicker you will be able to solve that problem. Also, if you have multiple methods for solving a single problem, then on the actual test when you "check over" your work you will be able to redo each problem in a different way. This will eliminate all "careless" errors on the actual exam. Note that in this book the quickest solution to any problem will always be marked with an asterisk (*).

2. The magical mixture for success

A combination of three components will maximize your SAT Math Subject Test score with the least amount of effort.

- Learning test taking strategies that work specifically for standardized tests.
- Practicing SAT Math Subject Test problems for a small amount of time each day for about one to two months before the test.
- Taking about two practice tests before test day to make sure you are applying the strategies effectively under timed conditions.

I will discuss each of these three components in a bit more detail.

Strategy: The more SAT specific strategies that you know the better off you will be. Throughout this book you will see many strategies being used. Some examples of basic strategies are "plugging in answer choices," "taking guesses," and "picking numbers." Some more advanced strategies include "identifying arithmetic sequences with linear equations," and "recognizing special triangles inside circles." Pay careful attention to as many strategies as possible and try to internalize them. Even if you do not need to use a strategy for that specific problem, you will certainly find it useful for other problems in the future.

Practice: The problems given in this book are more than enough to vastly improve your current SAT Math Subject Test score. All you need to do is work on these problems for about twenty minutes each day over a period of one to two months and the final result will far exceed your expectations.

Let me further break this component into two subcomponents – **topic** and **level**.

      Topic: You want to practice each of the five general math topics given on the SAT Math Subject Test and improve in each independently. The five topics are **Number Theory, Algebra and Functions, Geometry, Probability and Statistics**, and **Trigonometry**. The problem sets in this book are broken into these five topics.

      Level: You will make the best use of your time by primarily practicing problems that are at and slightly above your current ability level. For example, if you are struggling with Level 2 Geometry problems, then it makes no sense at all to practice Level 5 Geometry problems. Keep working on Level 2 until you are comfortable, and then slowly move up to Level 3. Maybe you should never attempt those Level 5 problems. You can actually get an 800 on the Level 2 Subject Test without answering any of them.

Tests: You want to take about two practice tests before test day to make sure that you are implementing strategies correctly and using your time wisely under pressure. For this task you should use actual SAT Math Subject Tests such as those found in "The Official SAT Subject Tests in Mathematics Levels 1 and 2 Study Guide." Take one test every few weeks to make sure that you are implementing all the strategies you have learned correctly under timed conditions.

3. Practice problems of the appropriate level

In this book SAT Math Subject Test questions have been split into 5 Levels. Roughly speaking, the questions increase in difficulty as you progress from question 1 to question 50. So you can think of the first 10 problems as Level 1, the next 10 as Level 2 and so on.

Keep track of your current ability level so that you know the types of problems you should focus on. If you are still getting most Level 2 Geometry questions wrong, then do not move on to Level 3 Geometry until you start getting more Level 2 Geometry questions right on your own.

If you really want to refine your studying, then you should keep track of your ability level in each of the five major categories of problems:

- **Number Theory**
- **Algebra and Functions**
- **Probability and Statistics**
- **Geometry**
- **Trigonometry**

If you are stronger in Number Theory than Geometry, then it is okay to practice Level 4 Number Theory problems while you continue to practice Level 2 Geometry problems.

4. Practice a small amount every day

Ideally you want to practice doing SAT Math Subject Test problems about twenty minutes each day beginning one to two months before the exam. You will retain much more of what you study if you study in short bursts than if you try to tackle everything at once.

The only exception is on a day you do a practice test. You should do at least two practice tests before you take the test. Ideally you should do your practice tests on a Saturday or Sunday morning.

So try to choose about a twenty-minute block of time that you will dedicate to practice every night. Make it a habit. The results are well worth this small time commitment.

10

5. Redo the problems you get wrong over and over and over until you get them right

If you get a problem wrong, and never attempt the problem again, then it is extremely unlikely that you will get a similar problem correct if it appears on the SAT Math Subject Test.

Most students will read an explanation of the solution, or have someone explain it to them, and then never look at the problem again. This is *not* how you optimize your score. To be sure that you will get a similar problem correct on the actual test, you must get the problem correct before taking the real test—and without actually remembering the problem.

This means that after getting a problem incorrect, you should go over and understand why you got it wrong, wait at least a few days, then attempt the same problem again. If you get it right, you can cross it off your list of problems to review. If you get it wrong, keep revisiting it every few days until you get it right. Your score *does not* improve by getting problems correct. **Your score improves when you learn from your mistakes.**

6. Check your answers properly

When you go back to check your earlier answers for careless errors *do not* simply look over your work to try to catch a mistake. This is usually a waste of time. Always redo the problem without looking at any of your previous work. Ideally, you want to use a different method than you used the first time.

For example, if you solved the problem by picking numbers the first time, try to solve it algebraically the second time, or at the very least pick different numbers. If you do not know, or are not comfortable with a different method, then use the same method, but do the problem from the beginning and do not look at your original solution. If your two answers do not match up, then you know that this a problem you need to spend a little more time on to figure out where your error is.

This may seem time consuming, but that's ok. It is better to spend more time checking over a few problems than to rush through a lot of problems and repeat the same mistakes.

11

7. Guess when appropriate

Answering a multiple choice question wrong will result in a 1/4-point penalty. This is to discourage random guessing. If you have no idea how to do a problem, no intuition as to what the correct answer might be, and you can't even eliminate a single answer choice, then *DO NOT* just take a guess. Omit the question and move on.

If, however, you can eliminate even one answer choice, you should take a guess from the remaining four. You should of course eliminate as many choices as you can before you take your guess.

8. Pace yourself

Do not waste your time on a question that is too hard or will take too long. After you've been working on a question for about 30 to 45 seconds you need to make a decision. If you understand the question and think that you can get the answer in another 30 seconds or so, continue to work on the problem. If you still do not know how to do the problem or you are using a technique that is going to take a long time, mark it off and come back to it later if you have time.

If you do not know the correct answer, but you can eliminate at least one answer choice, then take a guess. But you still want to leave open the possibility of coming back to it later. Remember that every problem is worth the same amount. Do not sacrifice problems that you may be able to do by getting hung up on a problem that is too hard for you.

9. Attempt the right number of questions

Many students make the mistake of thinking that they have to attempt every single question on the SAT Subject Tests. There is no such rule. In fact, most students will increase their score by *reducing* the number of questions they attempt.

Keep in mind that the questions on the test tend to start out easier in the beginning of the section and get harder as you go. Therefore, you should not rush through earlier questions in an attempt to get through the whole test. That said, it is okay to skip several questions that you are stuck on and try a few that appear later on.

Note that although the questions tend to get harder as you go, it is not true that each question is harder than the previous question. For example, it is possible for question 25 to be easier than question 24, and in fact, question 25 can even be easier than question 20. But it is unlikely that question 50 would be easier than question 20.

If you are particularly strong in a certain subject area, then you may want to "seek out" questions from that topic even though they may be more difficult. For example, if you are very strong at number theory problems, but very weak at probability problems, then you may want to try every number theory problem no matter where it appears, and you may want to reduce the number of probability problems you attempt.

10. Use your calculator wisely.

- Use a TI-84 or comparable calculator if possible when practicing and during the SAT Subject Test.
- Make sure that your calculator has fresh batteries on test day.
- You may have to switch between DEGREE and RADIAN modes during the test. If you are using a TI-84 (or equivalent) calculator press the MODE button and scroll down to the third line when necessary to switch between modes.

Below are the most important things you should practice on your graphing calculator.

- Practice entering complicated computations in a single step.
- Know when to insert parentheses:
    - Around numerators of fractions
    - Around denominators of fractions
    - Around exponents
    - Whenever you actually see parentheses in the expression

Examples:

We will substitute a 5 in for x in each of the following examples.

Expression	Calculator computation
$\dfrac{7x+3}{2x-11}$	$(7*5 + 3)/(2*5 - 11)$
$(3x-8)^{2x-9}$	$(3*5 - 8)\wedge(2*5 - 9)$

- Clear the screen before using it in a new problem. The big screen allows you to check over your computations easily.
- Press the **ANS** button (**2ND (-)**) to use your last answer in the next computation.
- Press **2ND ENTER** to bring up your last computation for editing. This is especially useful when you are plugging in answer choices, or guessing and checking.

- You can press **2ND ENTER** over and over again to cycle backwards through all the computations you have ever done.
- Know where the $\sqrt{\ }$, π, ^, e^x, **LOG** and **LN** buttons are so you can reach them quickly.
- Change a decimal to a fraction by pressing **MATH ENTER ENTER**.
- Press the **MATH** button - in the first menu that appears you can take cube roots and nth roots for any n. Scroll right to **NUM** and you have **lcm(** and **gcd(**. Scroll right to **PRB** and you have **nPr**, **nCr**, and **!** to compute permutations, combinations and factorials very quickly.
- Know how to use the **SIN**, **COS** and **TAN** buttons as well as **SIN^{-1}**, **COS^{-1}** and **TAN^{-1}**.

You may find the following graphing tools useful.

- Press the **Y=** button to enter a function, and then hit **ZOOM 6** to graph it in a standard window.
- Practice using the **WINDOW** button to adjust the viewing window of your graph.
- Practice using the **TRACE** button to move along the graph and look at some of the points plotted.
- Pressing **2ND TRACE** (which is really **CALC**) will bring up a menu of useful items. For example, selecting **ZERO** will tell you where the graph hits the x-axis, or equivalently where the function is zero. Selecting **MINIMUM** or **MAXIMUM** can find the vertex of a parabola. Selecting **INTERSECT** will find the point of intersection of 2 graphs.

PROBLEMS BY LEVEL AND TOPIC WITH FULLY EXPLAINED SOLUTIONS

Note: The quickest solution will always be marked with an asterisk (*).

LEVEL 1: NUMBER THEORY

1. Which of the following sequences of inequalities expresses a true relationship between $1, \frac{\pi}{2},$ and $\frac{e}{3}$?

   (A) $1 < \frac{\pi}{2} < \frac{e}{3}$

   (B) $1 < \frac{e}{3} < \frac{\pi}{2}$

   (C) $\frac{\pi}{2} < 1 < \frac{e}{3}$

   (D) $\frac{\pi}{2} < \frac{e}{3} < 1$

   (E) $\frac{e}{3} < 1 < \frac{\pi}{2}$

Solution by changing to decimals: We divide in our calculator to get

$$\frac{\pi}{2} = \pi / 2 \approx 1.57, \text{ and } \frac{e}{3} = e / 3 \approx .906.$$

Since $.906 < 1 < 1.57$, we have $\frac{e}{3} < 1 < \frac{\pi}{2}$, choice (E).

* Quick mental solution: Since $\pi \approx 3.14$, it is clear that $\frac{\pi}{2} > 1$. Since $e \approx 2.71$, it is clear that $\frac{e}{3} < 1$. So $\frac{e}{3} < 1 < \frac{\pi}{2}$, choice (E).

2. $\frac{7!}{4!-3!} =$

   (A) $5! + 4!$
   (B) $2(5! + 4!)$
   (C) $5! + 4! - 4$
   (D) $2(5! + 4! - 4)$
   (E) $2(5! + 4! - 3! + 2! - 1!)$

* We first use our calculator to compute $\frac{7!}{4!-3!} = 7! / (4! - 3!) = \mathbf{280}$.

We then start with choice (C) and compute

$$5! + 4! - 4 = 140.$$

15

Since this is half of the correct answer, the answer is choice (D).

Note: When plugging in or checking answer choices it is a good idea to start with choice (C) unless there is a specific reason not to. In this particular question it does not matter, but in some questions eliminating choice (C) allows us to eliminate two other answer choices as well.

Definition: The **factorial** of a positive integer n, written $n!$, is the product of all positive integers less than or equal to n.

$$n! = 1 \cdot 2 \cdot 3 \cdots n$$

$0!$ is defined to be 1, so that $n!$ is defined for all nonnegative integers n.

3. In an arithmetic sequence, the third term is 7 and the eighth term is 27. What is the tenth term in the sequence?

    (A) 35
    (B) 34
    (C) 33
    (D) 32
    (E) 31

* **Quick solution:** We can find the common difference of this arithmetic sequence with the computation

$$d = \frac{27-7}{8-3} = \frac{20}{5} = 4.$$

The ninth term is $27 + 4 = 31$, the tenth term is $31 + 4 = 35$, choice (A).

Remarks: (1) In an arithmetic sequence, you always add (or subtract) the same number to get from one term to the next. This can be done by moving forwards or backwards through the sequence.

(2) Questions about arithmetic sequences can easily be thought of as questions about lines and linear equations. We can identify terms of the sequence with points on a line where the x-coordinate is the term number and the y-coordinate is the term itself.

In the question above, since the third term of the sequence is 7, we can identify this term with the point $(3,7)$. Since the eighth term of the sequence is 27, we can identify this with the point $(8,27)$. Note that the common difference d is just the slope of the line that passes through these two points, i.e. $d = \frac{27-7}{8-3} = 4.$

Definition: An **arithmetic sequence** is a sequence of numbers such that the difference d between consecutive terms is constant. The number d is called the **common difference** of the arithmetic sequence.

Example of an arithmetic sequence: $-1, 3, 7, 11, 15, 19, 23, 27, 31, 35,\ldots$

In this example the common difference is $d = 3 - (-1) = 4$.

Note that this is the same arithmetic sequence given in this question.

Arithmetic sequence formula: $a_n = a_1 + (n - 1)d$

In the above formula, a_n is the nth term of the sequence. For example, a_1 is the first term of the sequence.

Note: In the arithmetic sequence $-1, 3, 7, 11, 15, 19, 23, 27, 31, 35,\ldots$ we have that $a_1 = -1$ and $d = 4$. Therefore,

$$a_n = -1 + (n - 1)(4) = -1 + 4n - 4 = -5 + 4n.$$

It follows that $a_{10} = -5 + 4(10) = -5 + 40 = 35$, choice (A).

Solution using the arithmetic sequence formula Substituting 3 in for n and 7 in for a_n into the arithmetic sequence formula gives us $7 = a_1 + 2d$.

Similarly, substituting 8 in for n and 27 in for a_n into the arithmetic sequence formula gives us $27 = a_1 + 7d$.

So we solve the following system of equations to find d.

$$\begin{aligned}27 &= a_1 + 7d \\ 7 &= a_1 + 2d \\ \hline 20 &= 5d\end{aligned}$$

The last equation comes from subtraction. We now divide each side of this last equation by 5 to get $d = 4$.

Finally, we add 4 to 27 twice to get $27 + 4(2) = 35$, choice (A).

Remarks: (1) We used the elimination method to find d here. This is usually the quickest way to solve a system of linear equations on this test.

(2) Once we have that $d = 4$, we can substitute this into either of the original equations to find a_1. For example, we have $7 = a_1 + 2(4)$, so that $a_1 = 7 - 8 = -1$.

4. A deposit of $800 is made into an account that earns 2% interest compounded annually. If no additional deposits are made, how many years will it take until there is $990 in the account?

    (A) 9
    (B) 10
    (C) 11
    (D) 12
    (E) 13

* We use the formula $A = P(1 + r)^t$ for interest compounded annually. We are given that $P = 800$, $r = 0.02$, $A = 990$, and we want to find t. So we have $990 = 800(1.02)^t$. We can now proceed in 2 ways.

Method 1 – Starting with choice (C): We start with choice (C) and substitute 11 in for t to get $800(1.02)^{11} \approx 994.7$. So the answer is (C).

Note that $800(1.02)^{10} \approx 975$, and this is too small.

Method 2 – Algebraic solution: We divide each side of the equation by 800 to get $1.2375 = (1.02)^t$. We then take the natural logarithm of each side to get $\ln 1.2375 = \ln(1.02)^t$. We can now use a basic law of logarithms to bring the t out in front of 1.02 (see the last row of the table below). We get $\ln 1.2375 = t \ln 1.02$.

Finally, we use our calculator to divide $\ln 1.2375$ by $\ln 1.02$ to get $t \approx 10.76$. So it will take 11 years to get $990 in the account, choice (C).

Laws of Logarithms: Here is a review of the basic laws of logarithms.

Law	Example
$\log_b 1 = 0$	$\log_2 1 = 0$
$\log_b b = 1$	$\log_6 6 = 1$
$\log_b x + \log_b y = \log_b(xy)$	$\log_5 7 + \log_5 2 = \log_5 14$
$\log_b x - \log_b y = \log_b(\frac{x}{y})$	$\log_3 21 - \log_3 7 = \log_3 3 = 1$
$\log_b x^n = n\log_b x$	$\log_8 3^5 = 5\log_8 3$

More general interest formula: For interest compounded n times a year we use the formula $A = P\left(1 + \frac{r}{n}\right)^{nt}$ where n is the number of compoundings per year. For example, if the interest is being compounded annually (once per year), then $n = 1$, and we get the formula used in the solution above. Other common examples are semiannually ($n = 2$), quarterly ($n = 4$), and monthly ($n = 12$).

LEVEL 1: ALGEBRA AND FUNCTIONS

5. $w\left(\frac{3}{5t} - \frac{1}{u}\right) =$

  (A) $\dfrac{2}{5tw - uw}$

  (B) $\dfrac{3uw - 5tw}{5ut}$

  (C) $\dfrac{2w}{5tu}$

  (D) $\dfrac{2w}{5t - u}$

  (E) $\dfrac{3w}{5tu}$

Solution by picking numbers: Let's let $w = 5$, $t = 2$ and $u = 10$. Then $w\left(\frac{3}{5t} - \frac{1}{u}\right) = 5\left(\frac{3}{10} - \frac{1}{10}\right) = 5\left(\frac{2}{10}\right) = \mathbf{1}$. Put a nice big, dark circle around **1** so you can find it easily later. We now substitute our values for w, t and u into each answer choice.

  (A) $\dfrac{2}{50 - 50} =$ undefined

  (B) $\dfrac{150 - 50}{100} = 1$

  (C) $\dfrac{10}{100} = 0.1$

  (D) $\dfrac{10}{10 - 10} =$ undefined

  (E) $\dfrac{15}{100} = 0.15$

Since A, C, D and E are incorrect we can eliminate them. Therefore, the answer is choice (B).

* Algebraic solution: We have $w\left(\frac{3}{5t} - \frac{1}{u}\right) = w\left(\frac{3u}{5ut} - \frac{5t}{5ut}\right) = \frac{3uw - 5tw}{5ut}$. This is choice (B).

Notes: (1) To get from the first expression to the second we note that the the **least common denominator** is $5ut$. Since $\frac{3}{5t}$ already has $5t$ in the denominator we only need to multiply the denominator and numerator by u to get $\frac{3}{5t} \cdot \frac{u}{u} = \frac{3u}{5ut}$. Similarly, since $\frac{1}{u}$ already has u in the denominator we only need to multiply the denominator and numerator by $5t$ to get $\frac{1}{u} \cdot \frac{5t}{5t} = \frac{5t}{5ut}$.

19

(2) To get from the second expression to the third we first rewrite $\frac{3u}{5ut} - \frac{5t}{5ut}$ as $\frac{3u-5t}{5ut}$. We then distribute the w to get $\frac{3uw-5tw}{5ut}$.

6. If $2x + 3y = 5$, $2y + z = 3$, and $x + 5y + z = 3$, then $x =$

    (A) 1
    (B) 3
    (C) 4
    (D) 5
    (E) 7

* Solution by performing simple operations: We add the first two equations and subtract the second equation to get $x = 5 + 3 - 3 = 5$, choice (D).

Computations in detail: We add the first two equations:

$$\begin{array}{r} 2x + 3y = 5 \\ 2y + z = 3 \\ \hline 2x + 5y + z = 8 \end{array}$$

We then subtract the third equation from this result:

$$\begin{array}{r} 2x + 5y + z = 8 \\ x + 5y + z = 3 \\ \hline x = 5 \end{array}$$

Solution using Gauss-Jordan reduction: Push the MATRIX button, scroll over to EDIT and then select [A] (or press 1). We will be inputting a 3×4 matrix, so press 3 ENTER 4 ENTER. Then enter the numbers 2, 3, 0 and 5 for the first row, 0, 2, 1 and 3 for the second row, and 1, 5, 1 and 3 for the third row.

Now push the QUIT button (2ND MODE) to get a blank screen. Press MATRIX again. This time scroll over to MATH and select rref((or press B). Then press MATRIX again and select [A] (or press 1) and press ENTER.

The display will show the following.

$$\begin{bmatrix} [1\,0\,0 & 5 \ ] \\ [0\,1\,0 & -1.67\,] \\ [0\,0\,1 & 6.33\,]] \end{bmatrix}$$

The first line is interpreted as $x = 5$, choice (D).

20

Notes: (1) In the first paragraph of this solution we created the **augmented matrix** for the system of equations. This is simply an array of numbers which contains the coefficients of the variables together with the right hand sides of the equations.

(2) In the second paragraph we put the matrix into **reduced row echelon form** (rref). In this form we can read off the solution to the original system of equations.

Warning: Be careful to use the rref(button (2 r's), and not the ref(button (which has only one r).

7. If $\sqrt{7b^3} = 3.27$, then $b =$

    (A) .43
    (B) 1.15
    (C) 1.53
    (D) 1.76
    (E) 12.66

* **Algebraic/calculator solution:** We square each side of the equation to get $7b^3 = 10.6929$. We then divide each side of this last equation by 7 to get $b^3 \approx 1.5276$. Finally, we take the cube root of each side of the last equation to get $b \approx 1.15$, choice (B).

Notes: (1) To take a cube root in your calculator you can either use the cube root function found in the MATH menu, or raise the number to the $\frac{1}{3}$ power. In this example you would type 1.5276 ^ (1 / 3) ENTER, or even better just use the calculator's previous answer and type ^ (1 / 3) ENTER.

(2) When possible try to get in the habit of using the calculator's previous answer instead of retyping decimal approximations. For example, this problem can be solved by pressing the following sequence of buttons:

$$3.27 \wedge 2 / 7 \text{ ENTER} \wedge (1 / 3) \text{ ENTER}$$

8. If $k(x) = \frac{x^2-1}{x+2}$ and $h(x) = \ln x^2$, then $k(h(e)) =$

    (A) 0.12
    (B) 0.50
    (C) 0.51
    (D) 0.75
    (E) 1.25

* Quick solution: $h(e) = \ln e^2 = 2$. So $k(h(e)) = k(2) = \frac{2^2-1}{2+2} = 0.75$, choice (D).

Notes: (1) We first substituted e into the function h to get 2. We then substituted 2 into the function k to get 0.75.

(2) The word "logarithm" just means "exponent."

(3) The equation $y = \log_b x$ can be read as "y is the exponent when we rewrite x with a base of b." In other words, we are raising b to the power y. So the equation can be written in exponential form as $x = b^y$.

(4) There are several ways to compute $\ln e^2$.

Method 1: Simply use your calculator.

Method 2: Recall that the functions e^x and $\ln x$ are inverses of each other. This means that $e^{\ln x} = x$ and $\ln e^x = x$. Substituting $x = 2$ into the second equation gives the desired result.

Method 3: Remember that $\ln x = \log_e x$. So we can rewrite the equation $y = \ln e^2$ in exponential form as $e^y = e^2$. So $y = 2$.

Method 4: Recall that $\ln e = 1$. We have $\ln e^2 = 2 \ln e = 2(1) = 2$. Here we have used the last law in the table at the end of the solution to problem 4.

(5) The base b of a logarithm must satisfy $b > 0$ and $b \neq 1$.

9. If -7 and 5 are both zeros of the polynomial $q(x)$, then a factor of $q(x)$ is

   (A) $x^2 - 35$
   (B) $x^2 + 35$
   (C) $x^2 + 2x + 35$
   (D) $x^2 - 2x + 35$
   (E) $x^2 + 2x - 35$

* Algebraic solution: $(x + 7)$ and $(x - 5)$ are both factors of $q(x)$. Therefore, so is $(x + 7)(x - 5) = x^2 + 2x - 35$, choice (E).

Note: There are several ways to multiply two binomials. One way familiar to many students is by FOILing. If you are comfortable with the method of FOILing you can use it here, but an even better way is to use the same algorithm that you already know for multiplication of whole numbers.

$$x + 7$$
$$\underline{x - 5}$$
$$-5x - 35$$
$$\underline{x^2 + 7x + 0}$$
$$x^2 + 2x - 35$$

What we did here is mimic the procedure for ordinary multiplication. We begin by multiplying –5 by 7 to get –35. We then multiply –5 by x to get –5x. This is where the first row under the first line comes from.

Next we put 0 in as a placeholder on the next line. We then multiply x by 7 to get 7x. And then we multiply x by x to get x^2. This is where the second row under the first line comes from.

Now we add the two rows to get $x^2 + 2x - 35$.

Solution by starting with choice (C): We are looking for the expression that gives 0 when we substitute in –7 and 5 for x.

Starting with choice (C) we have $5^2 + 2(5) + 35 = 70$. So we eliminate choice (C).

For choice (D) we have $5^2 - 2(5) + 35 = 50$. So we eliminate choice (D).

For choice (E) we have $5^2 + 2(5) - 35 = 0$ and $(-7)^2 + 2(-7) - 35 = 0$. So the answer is (E).

Notes: (1) c is a zero of a function $f(x)$ if $f(c) = 0$. For example, 5 is a zero of $x^2 + 2x - 35$ because $5^2 + 2(5) - 35 = 0$.

(2) A **polynomial** has the form $a_n x^n + a_{n-1} x^{n-1} + \cdots + a_1 x + a_0$ where $a_0, a_1, \ldots, a_n$ are real numbers. For example, $x^2 + 2x - 35$ is a polynomial.

(3) $p(c) = 0$ if and only if $x - c$ is a factor of the polynomial $p(x)$.

10. If $g(x) = x^2 - 3$ and $g(f(2)) = -2$, then $f(x)$ could be

(A) $x^3 - x^2 + x - 3$
(B) $x^3 - x^2 - 3$
(C) $x^3 + x - 3$
(D) $x^2 + x - 3$
(E) $x + 3$

* **Solution by starting with choice (C):** We start with choice (C) and guess that $f(x) = x^3 + x - 3$. We then have $f(2) = 2^3 + 2 - 3 = 7$ and $g(f(2)) = g(7) = 7^2 - 3 = 46$. This is incorrect so we can eliminate choice (C).

Let's try choice (B) next and guess that $f(x) = x^3 - x^2 - 3$. It follows that $f(2) = 2^3 - 2^2 - 3 = 1$ and so $g(f(2)) = g(1) = 1^2 - 3 = -2$. This is correct. So the answer is choice (B).

11. If $5x^2 - 2x + 3 = \frac{2}{7}(ax^2 + bx + c)$, then $a + b + c =$

    (A) 15
    (B) 17
    (C) 19
    (D) 21
    (E) 23

* Letting $x = 1$, the left hand side of the equation is $5(1)^2 - 2(1) + 3 = 6$ and the right hand side is $\frac{2}{7}(a(1)^2 + b(1) + c) = \frac{2}{7}(a + b + c)$. So we have that $\frac{2}{7}(a + b + c) = 6$, and so $a + b + c = 6(\frac{7}{2}) = 21$, choice (D).

12. If $y = \frac{2}{3}(x + 7)$ and $z = y + 212$, then which of the following expresses z in terms of x ?

    (A) $z = \frac{2}{3}(x + 219)$

    (B) $z = \frac{2}{3}(x + 205)$

    (C) $z = \frac{2}{3}(x - 7) + 212$

    (D) $z = \frac{2}{3}(x + 7) - 212$

    (E) $z = \frac{2}{3}(x + 7) + 212$

* Simply substitute $\frac{2}{3}(x + 7)$ in for y in the second equation to get $z = \frac{2}{3}(x + 7) + 212$, choice (E).

Remark: This problem can also be solved by picking a number for x. I leave it to the reader to solve the problem this way.

LEVEL 1: GEOMETRY

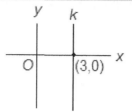

13. An equation of line k in the figure above is

    (A) $x = 3$
    (B) $y = 3$
    (C) $x = 0$
    (D) $y = x + 3$
    (E) $x + y = 3$

* A vertical line has equation $x = c$, where c is the x-coordinate of ANY point on the line. So the answer is $x = 3$, choice (A).

Note: Any equation of the form $y = a$ for some real number a is a horizontal line. Any equation of the form $x = c$ for some real number c is a vertical line. Horizontal lines have a slope of 0 and vertical lines have no slope (or to be more precise, **undefined** slope or **infinite** slope).

14. What is the distance between the points $(-2, 7)$ and $(3, -2)$

    (A) 14

    (B) $\sqrt{106}$

    (C) $\sqrt{26}$

    (D) $\dfrac{9}{5}$

    (E) $\dfrac{5}{9}$

* Solution using the distance formula:

$$d = \sqrt{\left(3 - (-2)\right)^2 + (-2 - 7)^2} = \sqrt{5^2 + (-9)^2} = \sqrt{25 + 81} = \sqrt{106}$$

This is choice (B).

Note: The distance between the points (s, t) and (u, v) is

$$d = \sqrt{(u - s)^2 + (v - t)^2}$$

Solution using the Pythagorean Theorem: We plot the two points and form a right triangle

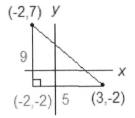

The legs of the triangle have lengths $7 - (-2) = 9$ and $3 - (-2) = 5$. By the Pythagorean Theorem, the hypotenuse of the triangle has length

$$\sqrt{9^2 + 5^2} = \sqrt{106}, \text{ choice (B)}.$$

15.   The intersection of a plane with a rectangular solid CANNOT be

(A) empty
(B) a point
(C) a line
(D) an ellipse
(E) a triangle

* **Solution by process of elimination:** If the plane is parallel to the rectangular solid the intersection can be empty. So we can eliminate choice (A). The plane can also touch a single vertex or a single edge of the rectangular solid, so we can eliminate choices (B) and (C). A diagonal slice through the solid can result in a triangle. So we can eliminate choice (E) and the answer is choice (D).

Visual explanation: The figure below shows a rectangular solid and three planes – one with empty intersection (A), one that intersects the solid in a point (B), and one that intersects the solid in a line (C). Can you draw a picture showing an intersection in a triangle?

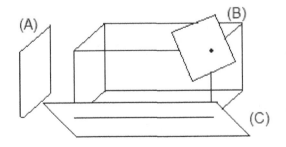

16. What is the surface area of a cube with a volume of 125 in³

    (A) 5 in²
    (B) 25 in²
    (C) 75 in²
    (D) 120 in²
    (E) 150 in²

* The length of an edge of the cube is $\sqrt[3]{125} = 5$ in. So the surface area of the cube is $6 \cdot 5^2 = 6 \cdot 25 = 150$ in², choice (E).

Some formulas: The **volume of a rectangular solid** is

$$V = lwh,$$

where l, w and h are the length, width and height of the rectangular solid, respectively.

In particular, the **volume of a cube** is $V = s^3$ where s is the length of a side of the cube.

The **surface area of a rectangular solid** is just the sum of the areas of all 6 faces. The formula is

$$A = 2lw + 2lh + 2wh$$

where l, w and h are the length, width and height of the rectangular solid, respectively.

In particular, the **surface area of a cube** is

$$A = 6s^2$$

where s is the length of a side of the cube.

17. In the rectangular coordinate system, the point $P(a, b)$ is moved to the new point $Q(5a, 5b)$. If the distance between point Q and the origin is k, what is the distance between point P and the origin?

    (A) $\dfrac{k}{5}$

    (B) k

    (C) $\dfrac{5}{k}$

    (D) $5k$

    (E) $25k$

Solution by picking numbers: Let's let $a = 1$ and $b = 2$. Then the points are $P(1,2)$ and $Q(5,10)$ and $k = \sqrt{5^2 + 10^2} = \sqrt{125} \approx 11.180$. The distance between P and the origin is $\sqrt{1^2 + 2^2} = \sqrt{5} \approx 2.236$. Put a nice big, dark circle around **2.236** so you can find it easily later. We now substitute our value for k into each answer choice.

(A) $\frac{11.180}{5} \approx 2.236$

(B) $k \approx 11.180$

(C) $\frac{5}{k} \approx .447$

(D) $5k \approx 55.9$

(E) $25k \approx 279.5$

Since B, C, D and E are incorrect we can eliminate them. Therefore, the answer is choice **(A)**.

* Direct solution: The distance between Q and the origin is

$$k = \sqrt{(5a)^2 + (10b)^2} = \sqrt{25a^2 + 100b^2}. = \sqrt{25(a^2 + b^2)}$$
$$= \sqrt{25}\sqrt{a^2 + b^2} = 5\sqrt{a^2 + b^2}$$

The distance between P and the origin is $\sqrt{a^2 + b^2} = \frac{k}{5}$, choice **(A)**.

Remark: These distances can also be computed by plotting points, drawing right triangles, and using the Pythagorean Theorem. See the second solution in problem 14 for details.

18. Which of the following is an equation of the line with an x-intercept of $(4,0)$ and a y-intercept of $(0,-3)$?

(A) $y = \frac{3}{4}x + 4$

(B) $y = \frac{3}{4}x - 3$

(C) $y = -\frac{3}{4}x + 4$

(D) $y = -\frac{3}{4}x - 3$

(E) $y = \frac{4}{3}x - 3$

* Solution by plugging in points: We plug in the given points to eliminate answer choices. Since the point $(0,-3)$ is on the line, when we substitute a 0 in for x we should get -3 for y.

28

(A) 4
(B) –3
(C) 4
(D) –3
(E) –3

So we can eliminate choices A and C.

Since the point (4,0) is on the line, when we substitute a 4 for x we should get 0 for y.

(B) $\frac{3}{4}(4) - 3 = 0$

(D) $-\frac{3}{4}(4) - 3 = -6$

(E) $\frac{4}{3}(4) - 3 \approx 2.33$

So we can eliminate choices (D) and (E), and the answer is choice (B).

Algebraic solution: We write an equation of the line in slope-intercept form. The slope of the line is $\frac{-3-0}{0-4} = \frac{3}{4}$. Since $(0, -3)$ is on the line, we have $b = -3$. So an equation of the line is $y = \frac{3}{4}x - 3$, choice (B).

Remark: We could have also gotten the slope geometrically by plotting the two points, and noticing that to get from $(0, -3)$ to $(4,0)$ we need to travel up 3 units and right 4 units. So the slope is

$$m = \frac{rise}{run} = \frac{3}{4}.$$

Slope formula and linear equations:

$$\text{Slope} = m = \frac{rise}{run} = \frac{y_2 - y_1}{x_2 - x_1}$$

Note: Lines with positive slope have graphs that go upwards from left to right. Lines with negative slope have graphs that go downwards from left to right. If the slope of a line is zero, it is horizontal. Vertical lines have **no** slope, or **undefined** slope (this is different from zero slope).

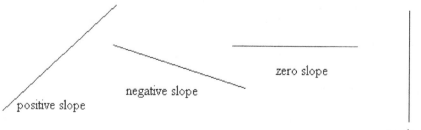

positive slope

negative slope

zero slope

no slope

The **slope-intercept form of an equation of a line** is $y = mx + b$ where m is the slope of the line and b is the y-coordinate of the y-intercept, i.e. the point $(0, b)$ is on the line. Note that this point lies on the y-axis.

19. How long is the minor axis of the ellipse whose equation is $\frac{(x-3)^2}{25} + \frac{(y+2)^2}{49} = 1$?

    (A) 5
    (B) 7
    (C) 10
    (D) 14
    (E) 25

* The length of the minor axis is $2a = 2 \cdot 5 = 10$, choice (C).

Notes: (1) In the given equation $a^2 = 25$, so that $a = 5$, and the length of the minor axis is $2a = 2 \cdot 5 = 10$.

(2) Here is a picture of this ellipse. The line segment labelled with length 5 is half of the minor axis.

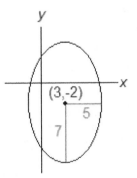

Ellipse facts: The standard form for an equation of an ellipse is

$$\frac{(x-h)^2}{a^2} + \frac{(y-k)^2}{b^2} = 1.$$

The **center** of this ellipse is (h, k). a is the horizontal distance from the center of the ellipse to a vertex of the ellipse, and b is the vertical distance from the center of the ellipse to a vertex of the ellipse. The lengths of the two **axes** of the ellipse are $2a$ and $2b$. The larger of these two numbers is the **major axis** and the smaller of these two numbers is the **minor axis**.

30

20. Lines k and n are perpendicular and intersect at (0,0). If line n passes through the point (–3,1), then line k does NOT pass through which of the following points?

   (A) (–2,–6)
   (B) (–1, –2)
   (C) (1,3)
   (D) (3,9)
   (E) (7,21)

* Line n has slope $\frac{1}{-3} = -\frac{1}{3}$ and therefore line k has slope 3. So an equation of line k is $y = 3x$. Since $-2 \neq 3(-1)$, the point $(-1, -2)$ is NOT on line k. So the answer is choice (B).

Remarks: (1) Here we have used the slope formula $m = \frac{y_2 - y_1}{x_2 - x_1}$.

(2) If the line j passes through the origin (the point $(0, 0)$) and the point (a, b) with $a \neq 0$, then the slope of line j is simply $\frac{b}{a}$.

(3) Perpendicular lines have slopes that are negative reciprocals of each other. The reciprocal of $-\frac{1}{3}$ is -3. The negative reciprocal of $-\frac{1}{3}$ is 3.

(4) Note that in answer choices A, C, D, and E, the y-coordinate of the point is 3 times the x-coordinate of the point.

LEVEL 1: PROBABILITY AND STATISTICS

21. The mean test grade of the 17 students in a geometry class was 66. When Johnny took a make-up test the next day, the mean test grade increased to 67. What grade did Johnny receive on the test?

   (A) 83
   (B) 84
   (C) 85
   (D) 86
   (E) 87

Solution by changing averages to sums: We change the averages (or means) to sums using the formula

$$\text{Sum} = \text{Average} \cdot \text{Number}$$

31

We first average 17 numbers. Thus, the **Number** is 17. The **Average** is given to be 66. So the **Sum** of the 17 numbers is $66 \cdot 17 = 1122$.

When Johnny takes his make-up test, we average 18 numbers. Thus, the **Number** is 18. The new **Average** is given to be 67. So the **Sum** of the 18 numbers is $67 \cdot 18 = 1206$.

So Johnny received a grade of $1206 - 1122 = 84$, choice (B).

22. In Bakerfield, 60% of the population own at least 1 cat. 20% of the cat owners in Bakerfield play the piano. If a resident of Bakerfield is selected at random, what is the probability that this person is a piano player that owns at least 1 cat?

(A) 0.12
(B) 0.15
(C) 0.33
(D) 0.37
(E) 0.80

* Let E be the event "owns at least 1 cat," and let F be the event "plays the piano." We are given $P(E) = .6$ and $P(F|E) = .2$. It follows that $P(E \cap F) = P(E) \cdot P(F|E) = (0.6)(0.2) = 0.12$, choice (A).

Notes: (1) To change a percent to a decimal, divide by 100, or equivalently move the decimal point two places to the left (adding zeros if necessary). Note that the number 60 has an "invisible" decimal point after the 0 (so that $60 = 60.$). Moving the decimal to the left two places gives us $.60 = .6$.

(2) "60% of the population own at least 1 cat" is equivalent to "the probability that someone from the population owns a cat is .6." This was written above symbolically as $P(E) = .6$.

Similarly, "20% of the cat owners in Bakerfield play the piano" is equivalent to "the probability that someone from Bakerfield plays the piano **given** that this person owns a cat is .2." This was written above symbolically as $P(F|E) = .2$. Note that the symbol | is read "given," so that $P(F|E)$ is read "the probability of F given E.

(3) $E \cap F$ is read "the **intersection** of E and F." It is the event consisting of the outcomes that are common to both E and F. In this problem a member of $E \cap F$ is a person from Bakerfield that owns at least 1 cat **and** plays the piano.

32

(4) $P(F|E)$ is called a **conditional probability**. The conditional probability formula is $P(E \cap F) = P(E) \cdot P(F|E)$.

23. If $A = \{1,2,3,4,5,6,7,8,9,10\}$ and $B = \{3,6,9,12,15\}$, what is the mean of $A \cup B$?

   (A) 5.33
   (B) 5.82
   (C) 5.96
   (D) 6.24
   (E) 6.83

* $A \cup B = \{1,2,3,4,5,6,7,8,9,10,12,15\}$. Therefore, the mean of $A \cup B$ is

$$\frac{1+2+3+4+5+6+7+8+9+10+12+15}{12} = \frac{82}{12} \approx 6.83, \text{ choice (E).}$$

Notes: (1) $A \cup B$ is read "the **union** of A and B." It is the set consisting of the elements that are in A or B or both.

(2) The **average (arithmetic mean)** of a list of numbers is the sum of the numbers in the list divided by the quantity of the numbers in the list.

$$\textbf{Average} = \frac{\textbf{Sum}}{\textbf{Number}}$$

24. How many committees of 5 people can be formed from a group of 10 people?

   (A) 5
   (B) 10
   (C) 50
   (D) 252
   (E) 30,240

* This is a **combination**. The answer is $_{10}C_5 = 252$, choice (D).

Remarks:

(1) This is a combination because it does not matter in what order we take the 5 people. We are simply putting the 5 people together into a group.

(2) We can compute $_{10}C_5$ very quickly on our calculator as follows: first type 10. Then under the Math menu scroll over to PRB and select nCr. Finally type 5 and press ENTER.

(3) The formula for $_{n}C_r$ is $\frac{n!}{r!(n-r)!}$. So $_{10}C_5 = \frac{10!}{5!5!} = 252$. (Note that this is included for completeness. You do not need to know this formula.)

LEVEL 1: TRIGONOMETRY

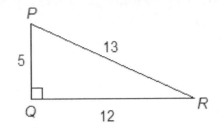

25. For $\angle R$ in $\triangle PQR$ above, which of the following trigonometric expressions has value $\frac{5}{12}$?

    (A) $\tan R$
    (B) $\cot R$
    (C) $\sin R$
    (D) $\csc R$
    (E) $\sec R$

Solution by plugging in answer choices: Let's start with choice C and compute $\sin R = \frac{\text{OPP}}{\text{HYP}} = \frac{5}{13}$. This is incorrect, but the numerator is correct. How do we make the denominator 12 instead of 13? Well we use tangent instead. Indeed, $\tan R = \frac{\text{OPP}}{\text{ADJ}} = \frac{5}{12}$. So the answer is choice (A).

Note: In the above solution, OPP stands for "opposite," ADJ stands for "adjacent," and HYP stands for "hypotenuse."

* **Quick solution:** Note that the numerator and denominator of the fraction are the lengths of the legs of the right triangle. So the answer is most likely a tangent or cotangent. Choices A and D look like the only candidates. Now we simply check: $\tan R = \frac{\text{OPP}}{\text{ADJ}} = \frac{5}{12}$. So the answer is choice **(A)**.

A quick lesson in **right triangle trigonometry** for those of you that have forgotten.

Let's begin by focusing on angle A in the following picture:

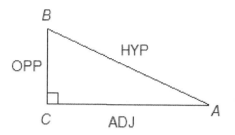

Note that the **hypotenuse** is ALWAYS the side opposite the right angle.

The other two sides of the right triangle, called the **legs**, depend on which angle is chosen. In this picture we chose to focus on angle *A*. Therefore, the opposite side is *BC*, and the adjacent side is *AC*.

Now you should simply memorize how to compute the six trig functions:

$$\sin A = \frac{\text{OPP}}{\text{HYP}} \qquad\qquad \csc A = \frac{\text{HYP}}{\text{OPP}}$$

$$\cos A = \frac{\text{ADJ}}{\text{HYP}} \qquad\qquad \sec A = \frac{\text{HYP}}{\text{ADJ}}$$

$$\tan A = \frac{\text{OPP}}{\text{ADJ}} \qquad\qquad \cot A = \frac{\text{ADJ}}{\text{OPP}}$$

Here are a couple of tips to help you remember these:

(1) Many students find it helpful to use the word SOHCAHTOA. You can think of the letters here as representing sin, opp, hyp, cos, adj, hyp, tan, opp, adj.

(2) The three trig functions on the right are the reciprocals of the three trig functions on the left. In other words, you get them by interchanging the numerator and denominator. It's pretty easy to remember that the reciprocal of tangent is cotangent. For the other two, just remember that the "s" goes with the "c" and the "c" goes with the "s." In other words, the reciprocal of sine is cosecant, and the reciprocal of cosine is secant.

To make sure you understand this, compute all six trig functions for each of the angles (except the right angle) in the triangle given in problem 25. Please try this yourself before looking at the answers below.

$$\sin P = \frac{12}{13} \qquad \csc P = \frac{13}{12} \qquad \sin R = \frac{5}{13} \qquad \csc R = \frac{13}{5}$$

$$\cos P = \frac{5}{13} \qquad \sec P = \frac{13}{5} \qquad \cos R = \frac{12}{13} \qquad \sec R = \frac{13}{12}$$

$$\tan P = \frac{12}{5} \qquad \cot P = \frac{5}{12} \qquad \tan R = \frac{5}{12} \qquad \cot R = \frac{12}{5}$$

35

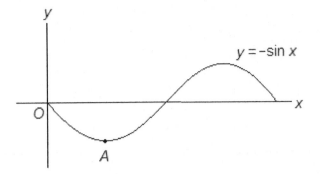

26. The figure above shows one cycle of the graph of the function $y = -\sin x$ for $0 \leq x \leq 2\pi$. If the minimum value of the function occurs at point A, then the coordinates of A are

(A) $(\frac{\pi}{3}, -\pi)$

(B) $(\frac{\pi}{3}, -1)$

(C) $(\frac{\pi}{3}, 0)$

(D) $(\frac{\pi}{2}, -\pi)$

(E) $(\frac{\pi}{2}, -1)$

* Let's add the key points into the figure.

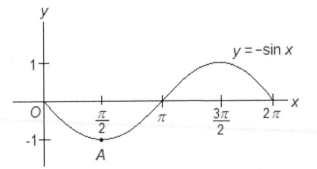

From this picture we can see that A has coordinates $(\frac{\pi}{2}, -1)$, choice (E).

36

27. In ΔDOG, the measure of $\angle D$ is 60° and the measure of $\angle O$ is 30°. If $\overline{DO}$ is 8 units long, what is the area, in square units, of ΔDOG ?

    (A) 4
    (B) 8
    (C) $8\sqrt{2}$
    (D) $8\sqrt{3}$
    (E) 16

* Solution using a 30, 60, 90 right triangle: Let's draw two pictures.

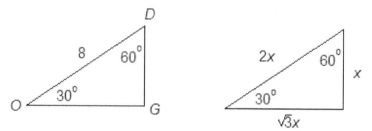

The picture on the left is what is given in the problem. Comparing this to the picture on the right we see that $x = 4$ and $\sqrt{3}x = 4\sqrt{3}$. So the area of the triangle is $\frac{1}{2}(4)(4\sqrt{3}) = 8\sqrt{3}$, choice (D).

Note: It is worth memorizing the 30, 60, 90 triangle on the right. You should also commit the 45, 45, 90 triangle to memory (see the end of the solution to problem 46 for details).

Trigonometric solution: We have $\sin 30° = \frac{DG}{8}$. So $DG = 8\sin 30°$. Similarly, $\cos 30° = \frac{OG}{8}$. So $OG = 8\cos 30°$. So the area of the triangle is $\frac{1}{2}(OG)(DG) = \frac{1}{2}(8\cos 30°)(8\sin 30°) \approx 13.8564$ (using our calculator). Now plug the answer choices into the calculator and we see that $8\sqrt{3} \approx 13.8564$, choice (D).

Remark: Make sure that your calculator is in degree mode. Otherwise you will get the wrong answer.

If you are using a TI-84 (or equivalent) calculator press MODE and on the third line, make sure that DEGREE is highlighted. If it is not, scroll down and select it.

28. If $0 \le x \le \frac{\pi}{2}$ and $\sin x = \frac{1}{5} \cos \frac{5\pi}{36}$, then $x =$

(A) 0.181
(B) 0.182
(C) 0.183
(D) 0.184
(E) 0.185

* **Calculator solution:** Make sure your calculator is in radian mode and type $\sin^{-1}$ (1 / 5 * cos (5π /36)). The display will read approximately 0.182269 which rounds to 0.182, choice (B).

Remark: Make sure that your calculator is in radian mode. Otherwise you will get the wrong answer.

If you are using a TI-84 (or equivalent) calculator press MODE and on the third line make sure that RADIAN is highlighted. If it is not, scroll down and select it.

29. Where defined, $\cos 3x \sec 3x =$

(A) $2 \csc 3x$
(B) $2 \sec 3x$
(C) -1
(D) 0
(E) 1

* **Quick solution:** Since $\sec x$ is the reciprocal of $\cos x$, the answer is 1, choice (E).

More detailed solution: $\cos 3x \sec 3x = \cos 3x \frac{1}{\cos 3x} = 1$, choice (E).

Reciprocal Identities: You should know the following,

$$\csc x = \frac{1}{\sin x} \qquad \sec x = \frac{1}{\cos x} \qquad \cot x = \frac{1}{\tan x}$$

Equivalently, we have

$$\sin x \csc x = 1 \qquad \cos x \sec x = 1 \qquad \tan x \cot x = 1$$

30. A dog, a cat, and a mouse are all sitting in a room. Their relative positions to each other are described in the figure below. Which of the following gives the distance, in feet, from the cat to the mouse?

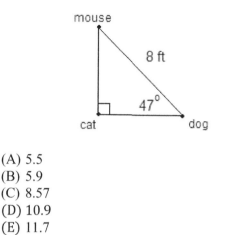

(A) 5.5
(B) 5.9
(C) 8.57
(D) 10.9
(E) 11.7

* Let x be the distance, in feet, from the cat to the mouse. Then we have $\sin 47° = \dfrac{\text{OPP}}{\text{HYP}} = \dfrac{x}{8}$. Multiplying each side of the equation $\sin 47° = \dfrac{x}{8}$ by 8 gives us $8\sin 47° = x$. So $x \approx 5.9$, choice (B).

Remarks: (1) If you do not see why we have $\sin 47° = \dfrac{\text{OPP}}{\text{HYP}}$, review the basic trigonometry given after the solution to problem 25.

(2) If you prefer, you can think of the multiplication above as **cross multiplication** by first rewriting $\sin 47°$ as $\dfrac{\sin 47°}{1}$.

So we have $\dfrac{\sin 47°}{1} = \dfrac{x}{8}$. Cross multiplying yields $8\sin 47° = 1x$. This yields the same result as in the above solution.

31. If $0 < x < \dfrac{\pi}{2}$ and $\sin x = 0.525$, what is the value of $\cos(\frac{x}{3})$

(A) 0.447
(B) 0.633
(C) 0.743
(D) 0.812
(E) 0.983

* $x = \sin^{-1} 0.525 \approx 0.553$. So $\cos(\frac{x}{3}) \approx \cos\left(\frac{0.553}{3}\right) \approx 0.983$, choice (E).

32. For any acute angle with measure A, $\sin(90° - A) =$

   (A) $\sin A$
   (B) $\cos A$
   (C) $\tan A$
   (D) $\csc A$
   (E) $\sec A$

Solution by picking a number: Let's let $A = 5°$. We use our calculator to get $\sin(90° - A) = \sin(85°) \approx \mathbf{0.996}$. Put a nice big, dark circle around **0.996** so you can find it easily later. We now substitute our value for A into each answer choice.

   (A) 0.087
   (B) 0.996
   (C) 0.087
   (D) 11.474
   (E) 1.004

Since A, C, D and E are incorrect we can eliminate them. Therefore, the answer is choice (B).

* Solution using an identity: We use the following difference identity:

$$\sin(x - y) = \sin x \cos y - \cos x \sin y$$

$$\sin(90° - A) = \sin 90° \cos A - \cos 90° \sin A$$

$\sin 90° = 1$ and $\cos 90° = 0$, so this last expression is $\cos A$, choice (B).

Cofunction Identities: You do not NEED to memorize these, but you can if you want:

$$\sin(90° - A) = \cos A \qquad\qquad \csc(90° - A) = \sec A$$

$$\cot(90° - A) = \tan A$$

LEVEL 2: NUMBER THEORY

33. What number should be added to each of the three numbers –2, 5, and 20 so that the resulting three numbers form a geometric progression?

>   (A) 8.125
>   (B) 8
>   (C) 7.875
>   (D) 7.5
>   (E) 7

* Algebraic solution: We want to find x so that $\frac{5+x}{-2+x} = \frac{20+x}{5+x}$. Cross multiplying gives us $(5 + x)^2 = (20 + x)(-2 + x)$. So we have

$$25 + 10x + x^2 = -40 + 18x + x^2$$
$$25 + 10x = -40 + 18x$$
$$65 = 8x$$
$$\frac{65}{8} = x$$

So $x = \frac{65}{8} = 8.125$, choice (A).

Notes: (1) If you are having trouble multiplying the binomials above, see the note at the end of the first solution to problem 9.

(2) A **geometric progression** is a sequence with a **common ratio**. This means that the quotient of any term with the preceding term always gives the same number.

(3) This problem can also be solved by "starting with choice (C)." I leave it to the reader to solve the problem this way.

34. If $a + b \le a - b$, then b is

>   (A) positive
>   (B) negative
>   (C) nonpositive
>   (D) nonnegative
>   (E) zero

* Algebraic solution: We subtract a from each side of the inequality to get $b \le -b$. Now we add b to each side of this last inequality to get $2b \le 0$. Finally, we divide by 2 to get $b \le 0$, choice (C).

41

Solution by picking numbers: Let's let $a = 2$ and $b = -3$. Then we have $a + b = 2 - 3 = -1$ and $a - b = 2 - (-3) = 5$. Since $-1 \leq 5$ the given condition is satisfied. So we can eliminate choices A, D, and E. If $b = 0$, we get $a \leq a$ which is true. So we can eliminate choice B. Therefore, the answer is choice (C).

35. What is the sum of the infinite geometric series?

$$\frac{1}{9} - \frac{1}{27} + \frac{1}{81} - \frac{1}{243} + \cdots ?$$

    (A) $\dfrac{1}{81}$

    (B) $\dfrac{1}{27}$

    (C) $\dfrac{1}{15}$

    (D) $\dfrac{1}{12}$

    (E) $\dfrac{1}{6}$

* The sum of an infinite geometric series with first term a and common ratio r with $-1 < r < 1$ is given by $\frac{a}{1-r}$. In this problem we have $a = \frac{1}{9}$ and $r = -\frac{1}{27} \div \frac{1}{9} = -\frac{1}{27} \cdot \frac{9}{1} = -\frac{1}{3}$. So the sum is $\frac{\frac{1}{9}}{1-\left(-\frac{1}{3}\right)} = \frac{\frac{1}{9}}{\frac{4}{3}} = \frac{1}{9} \cdot \frac{3}{4} = \frac{1}{12}$. This is choice (D).

36. If $\log_b 5 = 7$, then $b =$

    (A) 1.21
    (B) 1.26
    (C) 1.47
    (D) 1.73
    (E) 1.84

* We change the equation to the exponential form $b^7 = 5$ (see Note 3 at the end of problem 8). We now raise each side of this equation to the $\frac{1}{7}$ power to get $b = (b^7)^{\frac{1}{7}} = 5^{\frac{1}{7}} \approx 1.26$, choice (B).

Note: $(b^7)^{\frac{1}{7}} = b^{7 \cdot \frac{1}{7}} = b^1 = b$

Laws of Exponents: For those students that have forgotten, here is a brief review of the basic laws of exponents.

Law	Example
$x^0 = 1$	$3^0 = 1$
$x^1 = x$	$9^1 = 9$
$x^a x^b = x^{a+b}$	$x^3 x^5 = x^8$
$x^a / x^b = x^{a-b}$	$x^{11}/x^4 = x^7$
$(x^a)^b = x^{ab}$	$(x^5)^3 = x^{15}$
$(xy)^a = x^a y^a$	$(xy)^4 = x^4 y^4$
$(x/y)^a = x^a/y^a$	$(x/y)^6 = x^6/y^6$

LEVEL 2: ALGEBRA AND FUNCTIONS

37. If $a, b, c,$ and d are nonzero real numbers and if $a^3 b^6 c^{-11} d^{14} = \frac{7a^2 c^{-11}}{d^{-14}}$ then $ab^6 =$

   (A) $\frac{1}{7}$

   (B) 7

   (C) $7bcd$

   (D) $7c^{11}$

   (E) $7\frac{c^{11}}{d^{14}}$

* $ab^6 = a^3 b^6 c^{-11} d^{14} \cdot \frac{c^{11}}{a^2 d^{14}} = \frac{7a^2 c^{-11}}{d^{-14}} \cdot \frac{c^{11}}{a^2 d^{14}} = 7$, choice (B).

Remarks: (1) In order to change $a^3 b^6 c^{-11} d^{14}$ into ab^6 we multiply by c^{11} to cancel out c^{-11} and we divide by a^2 and d^{14} to cancel out d^{14} in the numerator and to change a^3 into a.

(2) $c^{-11} \cdot c^{11} = c^{-11+11} = c^0 = 1$. Similarly, $d^{-14} \cdot d^{14} = 1$.

(3) $a^3 \cdot \frac{1}{a^2} = \frac{a^3}{a^2} = a^{3-2} = a^1 = a$.

(4) Take a look at the Law of Exponents table above this problem.

38. If $5 - \dfrac{2}{x} = 2 - \dfrac{5}{x}$, then $\dfrac{x}{3} =$

    (A) -3

    (B) $-\dfrac{1}{3}$

    (C) 0

    (D) $\dfrac{1}{3}$

    (E) $\dfrac{2}{3}$

* **Algebraic solution:** We add $\dfrac{5}{x}$ and subtract 5 from each side of the equation to get $\dfrac{3}{x} = -3$. We then take the reciprocal of each side to get $\dfrac{x}{3} = -\dfrac{1}{3}$, choice (B).

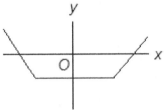

39. The graph of $y = h(x)$ is shown above. Which of the following could be the graph of $y = |h(x)|$?

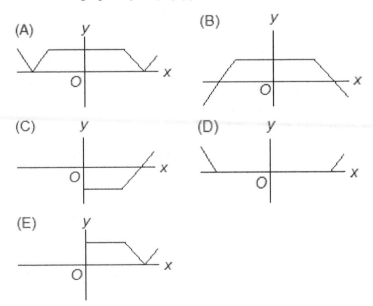

Recall that $|a|$ means the **absolute value** of a. It takes whatever number is between the two lines and makes it nonnegative. Here are a few examples: $|3| = 3, |-5| = 5, |0| = 0$.

* **Graphical solution:** To graph $|h(x)|$ from $h(x)$ simply leave the points that are above (and on) the x-axis exactly where they are, and reflect the points that are below the x-axis through the x-axis. So the answer is choice (A).

40. If $e^{x^2} = 5$, and $x > 0$, then $x =$

(A) 0.325
(B) 0.821
(C) 1.032
(D) 1.269
(E) 1.609

* **Algebraic solution:** Take the natural logarithm of each side to get

$$\ln e^{x^2} = \ln 5$$
$$x^2 = \ln 5$$
$$x = \sqrt{\ln 5} \approx 1.269, \text{ choice (D)}.$$

Notes: (1) Remember that $\ln k = \log_e k$.

(2) We can get from the first to the second equation by using one of the following methods:

Method 1: Recall that the functions e^x and $\ln x$ are inverses of each other. This means that $e^{\ln x} = x$ and $\ln e^x = x$. So $\ln e^{x^2} = x^2$.

Method 2: Recall that $\ln e = 1$. We have $\ln e^{x^2} = x^2 \ln e = x^2(1) = x^2$. Here we have used the last law in the table at the end of the solution to problem 4.

Solution by starting with choice (C): We start with choice (C) and use our calculator to compute $e^{\wedge}((1.032)^{\wedge}2) \approx 2.901$. This is too small so we can eliminate choices A, B and C.

Let's try choice (D) next. We get $e^{\wedge}((1.268)^{\wedge}2) \approx 4.992$. This looks close enough. So the answer is choice (D).

Remark: To be safe we can plug in choice (E) as well. We get $e^{\wedge}((1.609)^{\wedge}2) \approx 13.315$. This is too big confirming that the answer is (D).

45

41. What is the domain of $k(x) = \sqrt[3]{8 - 12x^2 + 6x - x^3}$?

    (A) All real numbers
    (B) $x < -2$
    (C) $-2 < x < 2$
    (D) $x > 2$
    (E) $x > 0$

* The domain of $f(x) = 8 - 12x^2 + 6x - x^3$ is all real numbers since $f(x)$ is a polynomial. The domain of $g(x) = \sqrt[3]{x}$ is also all real numbers. The function $k(x)$ is the composition of these two functions and therefore also has domain all real numbers. So the answer is choice (A).

Notes: (1) Polynomials and cube roots do not cause any problems. In other words, you can evaluate a polynomial at any real number and you can take the cube root of any real number.

(2) Square roots on the other hand do have some problems. We cannot take the square root of negative real numbers (in the reals). We have the same problem for any even root, and there are no problems for odd roots.

42. If $r(x) = \frac{7-6x}{3x-4}$, what value does $r(x)$ approach as x gets infinitely larger?

    (A) $-\frac{7}{4}$

    (B) -2

    (C) $\frac{7}{6}$

    (D) $\frac{4}{3}$

    (E) 2

Calculator solution: Simply plug in a really large value for x such as 999,999,999. We get (7 – 6 * 999,999,999) / (3 * 999,999,999) – 4) $= -2$. This is choice (B).

* **Quick solution:** For large x, $\frac{7-6x}{3x-4} \approx -\frac{6x}{3x} = -2$, choice (B).

Detailed solution: Note that as x gets infinitely large, $\frac{1}{x}$ approaches 0. We now divide each term in both the numerator and denominator by x to get $\frac{7-6x}{3x-4} = \frac{\frac{7}{x}-\frac{6x}{x}}{\frac{3x}{x}-\frac{4}{x}} = \frac{7\left(\frac{1}{x}\right)-6}{3-4\left(\frac{1}{x}\right)}$ which approaches $\frac{7(0)-6}{3-4(0)} = -\frac{6}{3} = -2$, choice (B).

Remark: Dividing each term by x is legal because it is equivalent to multiplying the fraction by $\frac{\frac{1}{x}}{\frac{1}{x}} = 1$. We do not have to worry about possibly dividing by 0 because we are assuming that x is very large.

43. If $g(f(x)) = \frac{5\ln(2^x+1)-2}{\ln(2^x+1)+3}$ and $g(x) = \frac{5x-2}{x+3}$, then $f(x) =$

 (A) $\ln x$
 (B) $\ln 2^x$
 (C) $\ln(2^x + 1)$
 (D) $\ln x^2$
 (E) $\ln(x^2 + 1)$

* Quick solution by observation: What do we replace x by in $g(x)$ to get $g(f(x))$? By observation the answer is $\ln(2^x + 1)$, choice (C).

Notes: (1) $g(f(x))$ is the **composition** of the function $g(x)$ with the function $f(x)$.

(2) We compute $g(f(x))$ by replacing x in the function $g(x)$ with $f(x)$. Since we do not know what $f(x)$ is in this problem, we must answer the question "what should I replace x by in the function $g(x)$?"

(3) If you do not immediately see what to replace x with in the function $g(x)$, use the answer choices as a guide. If you have no idea which one will work, then, as usual, you should begin by checking choice (C).

(4) If we are "guessing" that choice (C) is the answer, then we have that $g(f(x)) = g(\ln(2^x + 1)) = \frac{5\ln(2^x+1)-2}{\ln(2^x+1)+3}$. So choice (C) is correct.

44. If $h(x) = |7 - 2x|$, then $h(-3) =$

 (A) $h(-\frac{1}{3})$
 (B) $h(\frac{1}{3})$
 (C) $h(3)$
 (D) $h(7)$
 (E) $h(10)$

* We first compute $h(-3) = |7 - 2(-3)| = |7 + 6| = |13| = 13$.

We can now proceed in 2 ways:

47

Method 1 – Algebraic solution: We want to find the *other* solution of the equation $|7 - 2x| = 13$. So we set $7 - 2x = -13$ and solve for x to get

$$7 - 2x = -13$$
$$-2x = -20$$
$$x = 10$$

So we see that $h(10) = |7 - 2(10)| = |7 - 20| = |-13| = 13$. Therefore, the answer is choice (E).

Remarks: (1) Recall that $|a|$ means the absolute value of a. It takes whatever number is between the two lines and makes it nonnegative.

(2) The equation $|7 - 2x| = 13$ is equivalent to the two equations

$$7 - 2x = 13 \text{ and } 7 - 2x = -13.$$

The solution to the first equation is -3 and the solution to the second equation is 10.

Method 2 – Starting with choice (C): We start with choice (C) and compute $h(3) = |7 - 2(3)| = |7 - 6| = |1| = 1$. Since the answer is *not* 13, we can eliminate choice (C).

A little thought might suggest that a larger guess is required. If we try choice (E) next, we get $h(10) = |7 - 2(10)| = |7 - 20| = |-13| = 13$. So the answer is choice (E).

LEVEL 2: GEOMETRY

45. What is the distance in space between the points with coordinates (2,–5,–4) and (–3,2,3) ?

    (A) 8.7
    (B) 10.5
    (C) 11.1
    (D) 11.7
    (E) 12.3

* Solution using the distance formula in 3-space:

$$d = \sqrt{\left(2 - (-3)\right)^2 + (-5 - 2)^2 + (-4 - 3)^2}$$
$$= \sqrt{5^2 + (-7)^2 + (-7)^2} = \sqrt{25 + 49 + 49} = \sqrt{123} \approx 11.1$$

This is choice (C).

48

Note: The distance between the points (s, t, k) and (u, v, w) is

$$d = \sqrt{(u - s)^2 + (v - t)^2 + (w - k)^2}$$

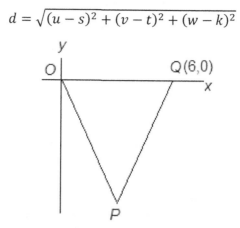

46. In the above triangle, if $OP = QP$ and $m\angle POQ = 60°$, what is the slope of segment PQ?

(A) $\dfrac{1}{\sqrt{3}}$

(B) $\dfrac{1}{\sqrt{2}}$

(C) $\sqrt{2}$

(D) $\sqrt{3}$

(E) $3\sqrt{3}$

* Let's add some information to the picture.

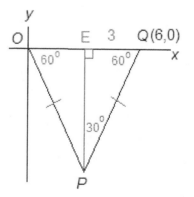

Note the following:

49

Since $OP = QP$, the triangle is isosceles. So $m\angle PQO = m\angle POQ = 60°$ (and therefore we also have $m\angle OPQ = 60°$) and line segment $\overline{PE}$ is the median, altitude and angle bisector. Since $\overline{PE}$ is a median, $EQ = \frac{1}{2} \cdot 6 = 3$. Since $\overline{PE}$ is an altitude, $m\angle PEQ = 90°$. And since $\overline{PE}$ is an angle bisector, $\angle EPQ = 30°$.

Since ΔPEQ is a 30, 60, 90 right triangle, $PE = 3\sqrt{3}$. It follows that the slope of segment PQ is $\dfrac{\text{rise}}{\text{run}} = \dfrac{3\sqrt{3}.}{3} = \sqrt{3}$, choice (D).

Notes: (1) See the end of problem 18 for more information on slope.

(2) A triangle is **isosceles** if it has two sides of equal length. Equivalently, an isosceles triangle has two angles of equal measure. A triangle is **equilateral** if all three of its sides have equal length. Equivalently, an equilateral triangle has three angles of equal measure (all three angles measure 60 degrees).

(3) An **altitude** of a triangle is perpendicular to the base. A **median** of a triangle splits the base into two equal parts. An **angle bisector** of a triangle splits an angle into two equal parts. In an isosceles triangle, the altitude, median, and angle bisector are all equal (when you choose the base that is **not** one of the equal sides).

(4) For the SAT Math Subject Test, it is worth knowing the following two special triangles:

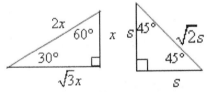

Some students get a bit confused because there are variables in these pictures. But the pictures become simplified if we substitute a 1 in for the variables. Then the sides of the 30, 60, 90 triangle are 1, 2 and $\sqrt{3}$ and the sides of the 45, 45, 90 triangle are 1, 1 and $\sqrt{2}$. The variable just tells us that if we multiply one of these sides by a number, then we have to multiply the other two sides by the same number. For example, instead of 1, 1 and $\sqrt{2}$, we can have 3, 3 and $3\sqrt{2}$ (here $s = 3$), or $\sqrt{2}, \sqrt{2}$, and 2 (here $s = \sqrt{2}$). For this problem, we are using the 30, 60, 90 right triangle and $x = 3$.

50

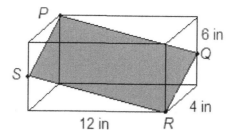

47. The figure above shows a rectangular solid with a length of 12 inches, a width of 4 inches, and a height of 6 inches. If points *S* and *Q* are midpoints of edges of the rectangular solid, what is the perimeter of the shaded region?

> (A) 14
>
> (B) 17.37
>
> (C) 34.74
>
> (D) 44.86
>
> (E) 68.92

* Note that region *PQRS* is a rectangle. We have *PS* = *RQ* = 5 since *RQ* is the hypotenuse of a triangle with legs of lengths 3 and 4 (3, 4, 5 is a Pythagorean triple).

$PQ = SR = \sqrt{3^2 + 12^2} = \sqrt{9 + 144} = \sqrt{153}$ by the Pythagorean Theorem.

So the perimeter of rectangle *PQRS* is $2(5) + 2\sqrt{153} \approx 34.74$, choice (C).

Notes: (1) The most common Pythagorean triples are 3,4,5 and 5, 12, 13. Two others that may come up are 8, 15, 17 and 7, 24, 25.

(2) The Pythagorean Theorem says that if a right triangle has legs of length *a* and *b*, and a hypotenuse of length *c*, then $c^2 = a^2 + b^2$.

(3) As stated in the solution above *RQ* is the hypotenuse of a right triangle with legs of lengths 3 and 4. The number 3 comes from the fact that *Q* is the midpoint of an edge of length 6. Similarly, *S* is also the midpoint of an edge of length 6.

48. Which of the following is an equation whose graph is the set of points equidistant from the points (2,5) and (7,5) ?

   (A) $y = 5$
   (B) $x = 5$
   (C) $y = 4.5$
   (D) $x = 4.5$
   (E) $y = x + 4.5$

Solution by drawing a picture: Let's draw a picture:

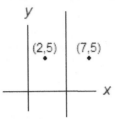

Notice that the set of points equidistant from (2,5) and (7,5) is the perpendicular bisector of the line segment from (2,5) to (7,5) (not shown). The x-coordinate of any point on this vertical line is the average of the x-coordinates of the two given points: $\frac{2+7}{5} = 4.5$. So the equation of this vertical line is $x = 4.5$, choice (D).

Note: See problem 13 for more information on vertical lines.

* Quick solution: The perpendicular bisector of the line segment from (2,5) to (7,5) is the vertical line $x = \frac{2+7}{2} = 4.5$, choice (D).

49. A sphere is inscribed in a cube with an edge of length 4. What is the volume of the space enclosed by the cube, but NOT by the sphere?

   (A) 15.1
   (B) 16.3
   (C) 18.9
   (D) 24.6
   (E) 30.5

* The volume of the cube is $V = s^3 = 4^3 = 64$. The radius of the sphere is half the length of an edge of the cube. So $r = 2$ and therefore the volume of the sphere is $V = \frac{4}{3}\pi r^3 = \frac{4}{3}\pi(2)^3 = \frac{32\pi}{3}$. The desired volume is then $V = 64 - \frac{32\pi}{3} \approx 30.5$, choice (E).

52

Remark: Here is a picture of the sphere inscribed in the cube.

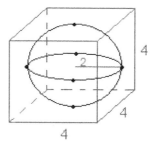

50. Which of the following is an equation of a line perpendicular to $3x + 2y = 5$?

    (A) $y = -\dfrac{3}{2}x + \dfrac{5}{2}$

    (B) $y = -\dfrac{3}{2}x + 1$

    (C) $y = \dfrac{3}{2}x + 1$

    (D) $y = \dfrac{2}{3}x + 1$

    (E) $y = -\dfrac{2}{3}x + 1$

* We first find the slope of the given line by putting it into slope-intercept form. In other words, we solve for y.

$$3x + 2y = 5$$
$$2y = -3x + 5$$
$$y = -\frac{3}{2}x + \frac{5}{2}$$

From this last equation we see that the given line has a slope of $-\dfrac{3}{2}$. So the slope of a line perpendicular to this one is $\dfrac{2}{3}$. Therefore, the answer is choice (D).

Notes: (1) See the end of problem 18 for more information on slope and slope-intercept form.

(2) Perpendicular lines have slopes that are negative reciprocals of each other. The reciprocal of $-\dfrac{3}{2}$ is $-\dfrac{2}{3}$. The negative reciprocal of $-\dfrac{3}{2}$ is $\dfrac{2}{3}$.

(3) The slope of a line in the **general form** $ax + by = c$ is $-\dfrac{a}{b}$. If you choose to memorize this fact, you can find the slope of the line given in

this problem quickly without first rewriting the equation in slope-intercept form.

In this question $a = 3$ and $b = 2$. So the slope of the line with equation $3x + 2y = 5$ is $-\frac{3}{2}$.

51. The vertices of rectangle R are (0,0), (0,4), (5,0), and (5,4). Let S be the rectangle that consists of all points $(3x, y - 2)$ where (x, y) is in R. What is the area of rectangle S?

(A) 20
(B) 30
(C) 40
(D) 60
(E) 84

Solution by drawing a picture:

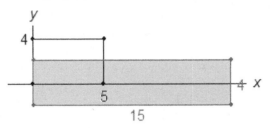

From the picture we see that the length of the new rectangle is 15 and the width is still 4. So the area is $(15)(4) = 60$, choice (D).

* **Quick solution:** The area of the original rectangle is $(5)(4) = 20$. We are expanding the rectangle in the x direction by a factor of 3, so the new area is $(20)(3) = 60$, choice (D).

Note: (1) The rectangle is being translated down 2 units. A translation does **not** change the area.

(2) A translation is an example of an **isometry**. An isometry is a transformation that preserves distances. Examples of isometries are translations, rotations and reflections.

(3) Dilations (expansions/contractions) are **not** isometries. In this problem there is a dilation in the x direction. Size is not preserved.

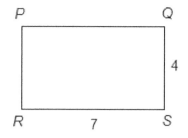

52. What is the volume of the solid generated by rotating rectangle *PQSR* around *PQ*?

    (A) 28π
    (B) 49π
    (C) 112π
    (D) 152π
    (E) 196π

* A cylinder is generated with base radius $QS = 4$ and height $RS = 7$. So the volume is $V = \pi r^2 h = \pi(4)^2(7) = 112\pi$, choice (C).

Here is a picture of the cylinder.

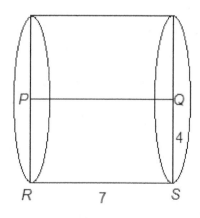

LEVEL 2: PROBABILITY AND STATISTICS

53. In how many different ways can 8 books be stacked in a pile?

(A) 8
(B) 64
(C) 40,320
(D) 322,560
(E) 16,777,216

Solution using the counting principle: There are 8 possible books for the bottom of the stack. After placing the first book, there are 7 possible books that can go on top of the bottom book, then 6, 5, 4, 3, 2 books, and finally 1 book for the top of the stack. By the counting principle we get $(8)(7)(6)(5)(4)(3)(2)(1) = 40{,}320$ arrangements, choice (C).

Note: The **counting principle** says that if one event is followed by a second independent event, the number of possibilities is multiplied.

More generally, if $E_1, E_2, \dots, E_n$ are n independent events with $m_1, m_2, \dots, m_n$ possibilities, respectively, then event E_1 followed by event E_2, followed by event E_3, ..., followed by event E_n has $m_1 \cdot m_2 \cdots m_n$ possibilities.

* Solution using permutations: There are 8 books, and we are arranging all 8 of them. So there are $_8P_8 = 8! = 40{,}320$ arrangements.

Remarks: (1) This is a permutation because we are arranging the books (stacking creates an arrangement).

(2) We can compute $_8P_8$ very quickly on our calculator as follows: first type 8. Then under the Math menu scroll over to PRB and select nPr. Finally type 8 and press ENTER. You will get an answer of 40,320.

(3) The formula for nPr is $\frac{n!}{(n-r)!}$. So $_8P_8 = \frac{8!}{0!} = 40{,}320$. (Note that this is included for completeness. You do not need to know this formula.)

54. In a small town, 30 families have cats, 50 families have dogs, and 15 families have both cats and dogs. If 25 families have neither cats nor dogs, how many families live in this town?

(A) 40
(B) 60
(C) 75
(D) 90
(E) 120

* **Quick computation:** Total = 30 + 50 − 15 + 25 = 90, choice (D).

Further explanation: We used the formula

$$\textbf{Total} = \textbf{\textit{C}} + \textbf{\textit{D}} - \textbf{\textit{B}} + \textbf{\textit{N}}$$

where C is the number of families that have cats, D is the number of families that have dogs, B is the number of families that have both, and N is the number of families that have neither. We are given that

$$C = 30, D = 50, B = 15, \text{ and } N = 25.$$

It follows that Total = 30 + 50 − 15 + 25 = 90, choice (D).

Solution by drawing a Venn Diagram: Let's draw a Venn diagram.

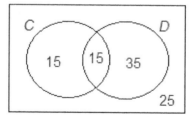

Note that we begin by putting 15 in the middle region. This region is $C \cap D$, the intersection of C and D. The 15 is the number of families that have both cats and dogs.

The leftmost 15 is the number of families that have cats only. We get this number by taking the 30 families that own cats and subtracting the number of families that have both cats and dogs. Similarly, the 35 comes from subtracting 15 from 50.

The 25 is the number of families that have neither cats nor dogs.

We get the total number of families by adding all the numbers in this diagram to get $15 + 15 + 35 + 25 = 90$, choice (D).

55. When a fair coin is flipped five times, what is the probability that the result will be exactly four heads?

   (A) $\dfrac{1}{32}$

   (B) $\dfrac{3}{32}$

   (C) $\dfrac{5}{32}$

   (D) $\dfrac{7}{32}$

   (E) $\dfrac{9}{32}$

* **Quick solution:** The total number of outcomes is $2^5 = 32$. The number of "successes" is 5. Therefore, the probability is $\dfrac{5}{32}$, choice (C).

Notes: (1) To compute a simple probability where all outcomes are equally likely, divide the number of "successes" by the total number of outcomes.

(2) In this problem there are 5 "successes," namely HHHHT, HHHTH, HHTHH, HTHHH, and THHHH.

(3) To compute the total we simply use the counting principle. Each time the coin is flipped there are 2 possibilities (heads or tails). So when the coin is flipped five times there are $(2)(2)(2)(2)(2) = 2^5 = 32$ possibilities. See the note at the end of problem 53 for information on the counting principle.

Solution using the binomial probability formula: The probability of an event with probability p occurring exactly r out of n times is

$$_nC_r \cdot p^r \cdot (1 - p)^{n-r}$$

In this question $n = 5$, $r = 4$, and $p = \dfrac{1}{2}$. So the desired probability is

$$_5C_4 \cdot \left(\tfrac{1}{2}\right)^4 \cdot \left(\tfrac{1}{2}\right)^1 = 5\left(\tfrac{1}{2}\right)^5 = \tfrac{5}{32}, \text{ choice (C).}$$

58

56. The set Q consists of 15 numbers whose arithmetic mean is zero? Which of the following must also be zero?

    I. The median of the numbers in Q.
   II. The mode of the numbers in Q.
  III. The sum of the numbers in Q.

    (A) I only
    (B) II only
    (C) III only
    (D) I and III only
    (E) I, II, and III

* Solution by using a specific list: Consider the following set:

$$\{-14, 1, 1, 1, 1, 1, 1, 1, 1, 1, 1, 1, 1, 1, 1\}$$

This set has an arithmetic mean of 0, but a median and mode of 1. So I and II do not need to be true. We can therefore eliminate choices A, B, D, and E. So the answer is choice (C).

Note: To see that III must be true recall the formula

Sum = Average · Number

Since the average (arithmetic mean) is zero, so is the sum.

LEVEL 2: TRIGONOMETRY

57. What is the range of the following function?

$$T(x) = 2\cos(3x - 2\pi) - 5$$

    (A) $3 \le y \le 7$
    (B) $-3 \le y \le 7$
    (C) $-3 \le y \le 2$
    (D) $-7 \le y \le 2$
    (E) $-7 \le y \le -3$

* The amplitude of $T(x)$ is 2 and there is a vertical shift of -5. So the minimum and maximum values of $T(x)$ are $-2 - 5 = -7$ and $2 - 5 = -3$. So the range is $-7 \le y \le -3$, choice (E).

Notes: (1) The **amplitude** of a function of the form $a\cos(bx + c) + d$ is $|a|$.

(2) The **vertical shift** of such a function is d.

(3) The **range** of such a function is $-|a| + d \leq y \leq |a| + d$.

(4) In this problem we do not need to worry about the **phase shift** $bx + c$.

(5) This problem can also be solved using the graphing functions on your TI-84 calculator. Make sure the calculator is in radian mode, enter the function under Y =, find a viewing window that captures the lowest and highest points of the function (you can start by pressing ZOOM 7 to get a standard trig window, and then change Ymin and Ymax under WINDOW to −10 and 0, respectively, for example), then use the minimum and maximum features under CALC to find the smallest and largest values in the range.

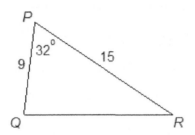

58. Triangle PQR is shown in the figure above. The measure of $\angle P$ is 32°, $PQ = 9$ in, and $PR = 15$ in. Which of the following is the length, in inches, of $\overline{QR}$?

(A) $9\sin 32°$
(B) $15\sin 32°$
(C) $\sqrt{15^2 - 9^2}$
(D) $\sqrt{15^2 + 9^2}$
(E) $\sqrt{15^2 + 9^2 - 2(15)(9)\cos 32°}$

* We use the law of cosines to get

$$QR^2 = 15^2 + 9^2 - 2(15)(9)\cos 32°$$

So $QR = \sqrt{15^2 + 9^2 - 2(15)(9)\cos 32°}$, choice (E).

Notes: (1) The **Law of Cosines** says $c^2 = a^2 + b^2 - 2ab\cos C$ where a, b, and c are the lengths of the sides of the triangle, and the side of length c is opposite angle C.

(2) This problem gives the most direct use of the law of cosines. In this example two side lengths of a triangle and the angle between these two sides are known. We are trying to find the length of the side opposite the known angle.

(3) Observe that QR is by itself on one side of the equation because it is opposite angle P.

59. If $\sin x = \cot x$, which of the following is a possible value of x ?

    (A) 0.542
    (B) 0.235
    (C) 0.00
    (D) −0.671
    (E) −0.905

* Solution using a graphing calculator: Make sure the calculator is in radian mode, and press Y=. Next to Y_1 type sin(X) and next to Y_2 type 1 / tan(X). Then press ZOOM 7 to get a standard trig window.

Press CALC (2ND TRACE) and select intersect (or press 5). The closest intersection points to the origin are approximately at $x = \pm 0.905$.

So the answer is choice (E).

Note: $\cot x = \dfrac{1}{\tan x}$. This is why we enter 1 / tan(X) for Y_2.

Solution by starting with choice (C): Make sure your calculator is in radian mode.

We start with choice (C) and guess that $x = 0$. We have $\sin 0 = 0$ and $\cot 0$ is undefined. So we can eliminate choice (C).

Let's try choice (D) next. We have $\sin(-0.671) \approx -0.622$ and $\cot -0.671 \approx -1.260$. So we can eliminate choice (D).

Let's try choice (E). $\sin -0.905 \approx 0.786$ and $\cot -0.905 \approx 0.785$. This is close enough. So the answer is choice (E).

Note: Since $\cot x$ is the reciprocal of $\tan x$, we can compute $\cot x$ in the calculator by computing $\tan x$ first, and then using the x^{-1} button. Alternatively, we can do this computation in one step by typing 1 / tan x.

Algebraic solution: Let's solve the equation algebraically.

$$\sin x = \cot x$$

$$\sin x = \frac{\cos x}{\sin x}$$

$$\sin^2 x = \cos x$$

$$1 - \cos^2 x = \cos x$$

$$0 = \cos^2 x + \cos x - 1$$

$$\cos x = \frac{-1 \pm \sqrt{1 - 4(1)(-1)}}{2(1)} = \frac{-1 \pm \sqrt{5}}{2}$$

$$x = \cos^{-1} \frac{-1+\sqrt{5}}{2} \approx 0.905$$

So 0.905 is one possible solution to $\sin x = \cot x$. Unfortunately, this is not an answer choice. But $\sin x$ and $\cot x$ are both odd functions. So -0.905 is also a solution, choice (E).

Notes: (1) Recall that $\sin^2 x$ is an abbreviation for $(\sin x)^2$. In other words, to compute $\sin^2 x$ we compute $\sin x$ first and then square the result. Compare this with $\sin x^2$ where we square x first and then evaluate the sine of the result.

Similarly, $\cos^2 x$ is an abbreviation for $(\cos x)^2$.

2) In going from the third equation to the fourth equation we used the Pythagorean identity $\cos^2 x + \sin^2 x = 1$ to replace $\sin^2 x$ by $1 - \cos^2 x$.

(3) Recall the quadratic formula: If $ax^2 + bx + c = 0$, then

$$x = \frac{-b \pm \sqrt{b^2 - 4ac}}{2a}.$$

(4) In going from the fifth equation to the sixth equation we used the quadratic formula to solve for $\cos x$. If you are having trouble seeing this, you may want to make the substitution $u = \cos x$ so that the equation becomes $0 = u^2 + u - 1$ with solution

$$u = \frac{-1 \pm \sqrt{1 - 4(1)(-1)}}{2(1)} = \frac{-1 \pm \sqrt{5}}{2}.$$

(5) A function f with the property that $f(-x) = -f(x)$ for all x in the domain of f is called an **odd** function.

A function f with the property that $f(-x) = f(x)$ for all x in the domain of f is called an **even** function.

$\sin x$ and $\tan x$ are odd functions and so are their reciprocals $\csc x$ and $\cot x$.

$\cos x$ is an even function and so is its reciprocal $\sec x$.

(6) Since $\sin x$ and $\cot x$ are odd functions, and $\sin 0.905 = \cot 0.905$, we have $-\sin 0.905 = -\cot 0.905$ and so $\sin(-0.905) = \cot(-0.905)$

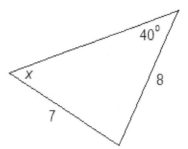

60. In the triangle shown above, $\sin x =$

(A) 0.175
(B) 0.265
(C) 0.523
(D) 0.735
(E) 0.825

* Solution using the Law of Sines: By the Law of Sines we have

$$\frac{\sin x}{8} = \frac{\sin 40°}{7}$$

So $\sin x = \dfrac{8 \sin 40°}{7} \approx 0.735$, choice (D).

The **Law of Sines** says $\dfrac{\sin A}{a} = \dfrac{\sin B}{b} = \dfrac{\sin C}{c}$ where A, B, and C are the angles in the triangle, and a, b, and c are the lengths of the sides opposite each of these angles.

61. If $0 \leq x \leq 2\pi$, $\tan x < 0$ and $\cos x \tan x > 0$, then which of the following is a possible value for x ?

(A) $\frac{\pi}{6}$

(B) $\frac{\pi}{2}$

(C) $\frac{5\pi}{6}$

(D) $\frac{7\pi}{6}$

(E) $\frac{11\pi}{6}$

* $\tan x < 0$ in Quadrants II and IV. Since $\cos x \tan x > 0$ we must have $\cos x < 0$. This is true in Quadrants II and III. So x must be in Quadrant II and therefore $\frac{\pi}{2} < x < \pi$. So the answer is choice (C).

Notes: (1) Many students find it helpful to remember the following diagram.

This diagram tells us which trig functions are positive in which quadrants. The **A** stands for "all" so that all trig functions are positive in the first quadrant. Similarly, **S** stands for "sine," **T** stands for "tangent," and **C** stands for "cosine."

So, for example, if angle x is in the second quadrant, then $\sin x > 0$, $\tan x < 0$ and $\cos x < 0$.

(2) The quickest way to see that $\frac{5\pi}{6}$ is between $\frac{\pi}{2}$ and π is to simply enter each number into your calculator and compare the decimal approximations.

62. If $0 \le x \le \frac{\pi}{2}$ and $\cos x = 5 \sin x$, what is the value of $\sec x$?

     (A) 0.36
     (B) 0.58
     (C) 0.87
     (D) 0.98
     (E) 1.02

* We divide each side of the equation by $\cos x$ to get $1 = \frac{5 \sin x}{\cos x} = 5\tan x$. So $\tan x = \frac{1}{5}$ and $x = \tan^{-1}\frac{1}{5}$. So $\cos x = \cos(\tan^{-1}\frac{1}{5}) \approx 0.98$. Therefore $\sec x = \frac{1}{\cos x} \approx 1.02$, choice (E).

Notes: (1) We can also begin by dividing each side by $\sin x$. We then get $\cot x = 5$. Since the TI-84 calculator does not have a button for cotangent, we then need to take the reciprocal of each side to get $\tan x = \frac{1}{5}$ as before.

(2) Recall that $\sec x = \frac{1}{\cos x}$.

63. $\tan^2 x + 1 =$

     (A) $\cot^2 x$
     (B) $\csc^2 x$
     (C) $\sec^2 x$
     (D) $\cos^2 x$
     (E) $\sin^2 x$

* Recall the Pythagorean identity $\cos^2 x + \sin^2 x = 1$. If we divide each side of this equation by $\cos^2 x$ we get the following.

$$\frac{\cos^2 x + \sin^2 x}{\cos^2 x} = \frac{1}{\cos^2 x}$$

$$\frac{\cos^2 x}{\cos^2 x} + \frac{\sin^2 x}{\cos^2 x} = \frac{1}{\cos^2 x}$$

$$1 + \tan^2 x = \sec^2 x$$

So $\tan^2 x + 1 = \sec^2 x$, choice (C).

Remarks: (1) $\cos^2 x + \sin^2 x = 1$ is the most important Pythagorean identity. Make sure you have this one memorized. You may also want to memorize the other two Pythagorean identities:

$$1 + \tan^2 x = \sec^2 x \quad \text{and} \quad \cot^2 x + 1 = \csc^2 x$$

As we saw in the solution above, the second Pythagorean identity is derived from the first by dividing each side of the first equation by $\cos^2 x$.

Similarly, the third Pythagorean identity is derived from the first by dividing each side of the first equation by $\sin^2 x$.

64. If $\cos x = 0.32$, then what is the value of $\frac{\sin x}{\cot x}$?

    (A) 1.96
    (B) 2.12
    (C) 2.34
    (D) 2.81
    (E) 2.98

* $x = \cos^{-1} 0.32$, and so $\frac{\sin x}{\cot x} = \frac{\sin(\cos^{-1} 0.32)}{\cot(\cos^{-1} 0.32)} \approx 2.81$, choice (D).

Note: There is no cotangent button on the TI-84 calculator. So we compute $\frac{\sin(\cos^{-1} 0.32)}{\cot(\cos^{-1} 0.32)} = \sin(\cos^{-1} 0.32) \cdot \tan(\cos^{-1} 0.32) \approx 2.81$.

LEVEL 3: NUMBER THEORY

65. A survey was taken from 114 cat owners in Addletown and 225 cat owners in Bergentown. A total of 113 cat owners from the two towns fed their cats "Tasties" cat food. If the same percentage of cat owners from each town used "Tasties," how many of the residents of Bergentown used "Tasties" cat food.

    (A) 72
    (B) 75
    (C) 77
    (D) 79
    (E) 81

* **Algebraic solution:** Let x be the number of residents from Bergentown that used "Tasties" cat food. It follows that $113 - x$ is the number of residents from Addletown that used "Tasties." Since the same percentage of cat owners from each town used "Tasties" we have

$$\frac{x}{225} = \frac{113-x}{114}.$$

We cross multiply to get $114x = 25{,}425 - 225x$.

We now add $225x$ to each side of this last equation to get $339x = 25{,}425$.

We divide each side of this equation by 339 to get $x = 75$, choice (B).

Notes: (1) If you do not see where $113 - x$ came from, here is a more detailed explanation: Let x be the number of residents from Bergentown that used "Tasties" cat food, and let y be the number of residents from Addletown that used "Tasties" cat food. We are given that a total of 113 cat owners from the two towns used "Tasties." So $x + y = 113$. It follows that $y = 113 - x$.

(2) Do not forget to check at the end that we have what we were being asked for. After finding x, note that we chose x to be the number of residents from Bergentown that used "Tasties." Since this is what is being asked for, $x = 75$ is the answer.

If we had started the problem by letting x be the number of residents from Addletown that used "Tasties," then x would not give the answer. We would need to find $113 - x$.

66. For some real number a, the first three terms of an arithmetic sequence are $6a - 3$, $8a + 3$, and $9a$. What is the common difference of the sequence?

   (A) 11
   (B) 7
   (C) –7
   (D) –11
   (E) –12

* Algebraic solution: We want to find a so that

$$(8a + 3) - (6a - 3) = 9a - (8a + 3)$$
$$8a + 3 - 6a + 3 = 9a - 8a - 3$$
$$2a + 6 = a - 3$$
$$a = -9$$

So the first two terms are $6(-9) - 3 = -57$ and $8(-9) + 3 = -69$, and therefore the common difference of the sequence is $-69 - (-57) = -12$, choice (E).

Remark: See problem 3 for more information about arithmetic sequences.

67. If $\log_b 2 = k$, then $\log_b 32 =$

    (A) $5k$
    (B) $16k$
    (C) $32k$
    (D) k^2
    (E) k^5

Solution by changing to exponential form: We change the equation to the exponential form $2 = b^k$ (see Note 3 at the end of problem 8). We now raise each side of this equation to the 5th power to get

$$32 = 2^5 = (b^k)^5 = b^{5k}. \text{ So } \log_b 32 = 5k$$

This is choice (A).

Note: See the table at the end of problem 36 for the law of exponents used here.

* Solution using logarithm laws: $log_b 32 = log_b(2^5) = 5log_b 2 = 5k$, choice (A).

Note: See the table at the end of problem 4 for the law of logarithms used here.

68. The only prime factors of the positive integer k are 3, 5, 7, 13, and 23. Which of the following could NOT be a factor of k ?

    (A) 15
    (B) 21
    (C) 91
    (D) 143
    (E) 299

* Solution by starting with choice (C): Let's start with choice C. If we start dividing 91 by each of 3, 5, 7, 13, and 23 we see that $91 = 7 \cdot 13$. So we can eliminate choice C.

Trying choice D next we see that $143 = 11 \cdot 13$. Since 143 has a prime factor of 11, 143 cannot be a factor of k. So the answer is choice (D).

Notes: (1) We are looking for an integer that has a prime factor other than 3, 5, 7, 13 and 23.

(2) Note that $15 = 3 \cdot 5$, $21 = 3 \cdot 7$ and $299 = 13 \cdot 23$. This eliminates choices A, B, and E.

LEVEL 3: ALGEBRA AND FUNCTIONS

69. If $f(x) = ax^3 + bx^2 + cx + d$ for all real numbers x and if $f(0) = 3$ and $f(2) = 5$, then $2a + b =$

   (A) 0
   (B) $\frac{1}{2}$
   (C) 2
   (D) $\frac{3-c}{4}$
   (E) $\frac{1-c}{2}$

* Since $f(0) = 3$ we have

$$3 = f(0) = a(0)^3 + b(0)^2 + c(0) + d = d.$$

Therefore $f(x) = ax^3 + bx^2 + cx + 3$.

Since $f(2) = 5$ we have

$$5 = f(2) = a(2)^3 + b(2)^2 + c(2) + 3 = 8a + 4b + 2c + 3.$$

Subtracting $2c + 3$ from each side of this equation yields

$$2 - 2c = 8a + 4b.$$

Finally, we divide each side of this equation by 4 to get

$$\frac{1-c}{2} = 2a + b.$$

So the answer is choice (E).

70. Which of the following lines is an asymptote of the graph of $y = \frac{1-x}{2+x}$?

   (A) $x = -1$
   (B) $x = 1$
   (C) $x = 2$
   (D) $y = -1$
   (E) $y = \frac{1}{2}$

69

* **Quick solution:** For large x, $y = \frac{1-x}{2+x} \approx \frac{-x}{x} = -1$ So $y = -1$ is a horizontal asymptote of the graph of the given function, choice (D).

Notes: (1) The horizontal line with equation $y = b$ is a **horizontal asymptote** for the graph of the function $y = f(x)$ if y approaches b as x gets larger and larger, or smaller and smaller (as in very large in the negative direction).

(2) A **polynomial** has the form $a_n x^n + a_{n-1} x^{n-1} + \cdots + a_1 x + a_0$ where $a_0, a_1, \ldots, a_n$ are real numbers. If $a_n \neq 0$, then n is the degree of the polynomial. For example, $1 - x$ is a polynomial of degree 1 (note that this polynomial can be written as $-x^1 + 1$).

(3) A **rational function** is a quotient of polynomials. The function given in this problem is a rational function.

(4) If a rational function consists of polynomials of the **same degree**, then the quick solution above gives a method for finding the only horizontal asymptote of the rational function.

(5) We can also find the horizontal asymptote by plugging in a really large value for x such as 999,999,999. We get

$$(1 - 999{,}999{,}999) / (2 + 999{,}999{,}999) = -0.999999997$$

which is practically -1.

(6) The vertical line $x = a$ is a **vertical asymptote** for the graph of the function $y = f(x)$ if y approaches $\pm\infty$ as x approaches a from either the left or right (or both).

(7) If the rational function $y = \frac{p(x)}{q(x)}$ has the property that $q(a) = 0$ and $p(a) \neq 0$, then $x = a$ is a vertical asymptote for the graph.

(8) In this problem plugging in -2 makes the denominator of the function 0 and the numerator nonzero. So $x = -2$ is a vertical asymptote for the graph of the given function. Note however that this is not an answer choice.

71. If $g(x^2 - 2) = x^4 - 4x^2$ for all real numbers x, $g(x)$ could be

    (A) x
    (B) $x + 1$
    (C) $x + 2$
    (D) $x^2 - 2$
    (E) $x^2 - 4$

* Solution by starting with choice (C): If $g(x) = x + 2$, then we have

$$g(x^2 - 2) = (x^2 - 2) + 2 = x^2.$$

So we can eliminate choice (C).

If $g(x) = x^2 - 2$, then

$$g(x^2 - 2) = (x^2 - 2)^2 - 2 = x^4 - 4x^2 + 4 - 2 = x^4 - 4x^2 + 2.$$

So we can eliminate choice (D).

If $g(x) = x^2 - 4$, then

$$g(x^2 - 2) = (x^2 - 2)^2 - 4 = x^4 - 4x^2 + 4 - 4 = x^4 - 4x^2.$$

So the answer is choice (E).

Note: (1) $(x^2 - 2)^2 = (x^2 - 2)(x^2 - 2) = x^4 - 2x^2 - 2x^2 + 4.$

(2) See the note at the end of the first solution to problem 9 for an alternative way to multiply polynomials.

72. If $K(x) = \log_5 x$ for $x > 0$, then $K^{-1}(x) =$

    (A) $\log_x 5$

    (B) $\frac{x}{5}$

    (C) $\frac{5}{x}$

    (D) x^5

    (E) 5^x

* Quick solution: The inverse of the logarithmic function $K(x) = \log_5 x$ is the exponential function $K^{-1}(x) = 5^x$, choice (E).

Notes: (1) In general, the functions $y = b^x$ and $y = \log_b x$ are inverses of each other. In fact, that is precisely the definition of a logarithm.

(2) The usual procedure to find the inverse of a function $y = f(x)$ is to interchange the roles of x and y and solve for y. In this example, the inverse of $y = \log_5 x$ is $x = \log_5 y$. To solve this equation for y we can simply change the equation to its exponential form $y = 5^x$.

(3) For more information on logarithms see problem 8.

73. What value does $\frac{\ln(x+1)}{e^x - 1}$ approach as x approaches 0 ?

(A) 0
(B) 1
(C) 2
(D) 4
(E) It does not approach a unique value

Calculator solution: Simply plug in a number really close to 0 for x such as .000001. We get $(\ln(.000001 + 1)) / (e\hat{\ }(.000001) - 1) \approx .99999$. This is essentially 1, choice (B).

* Solution using L'Hopital's Rule: $\lim\limits_{x \to 0} \frac{\ln(x+1)}{e^x - 1} = \lim\limits_{x \to 0} \frac{\frac{1}{x+1}}{e^x} = 1$, choice (B).

Notes: (1) This solution requires some knowledge of Calculus.

(2) The form of L'Hopital's rule here says that if a limit has the form $\frac{0}{0}$, then differentiating the numerator and denominator results in a function with the same limit as the original function.

(3) The derivative of a constant (a real number) is 0. For example, the derivative of -1 is 0.

(4) The derivative of e^x is e^x (that is e^x has its own derivative!).

(5) The derivative of $\ln x$ is $\frac{1}{x}$.

(6) The **chain rule** must actually be used to compute one of the derivatives in this problem, but a full explanation of this rule goes a bit too far outside of the scope of this book. So I will simply mention that the derivative of $\ln(x + 1)$ is $\frac{1}{x+1}$.

(7) Sums and differences can be handled term by term when taking derivatives. So the derivative of $e^x - 1$ is $e^x - 0 = e^x$.

(8) Note that substituting 0 in for x into the given function results in the following: $\frac{\ln(0+1)}{e^0 - 1} = \frac{\ln 1}{1-1} = \frac{0}{0}$. Here we have used the facts that $\ln 1 = 0$ and $e^0 = 1$.

(9) The form $\frac{0}{0}$ is called an indeterminate form. If you wind up with this form when plugging in a value to try to compute a limit, L'Hopital's rule can be applied.

(10) The other standard indeterminate form is $\frac{\infty}{\infty}$. L'Hopital's rule can be applied exactly the same way for this form.

Solution using the TABLE feature on a TI-84: Press Y= and enter ln(X + 1)/(e^(X) − 1) for Y_1. Press the TBLSET button (2ND WINDOW), set TblStart to 0, and ΔTbl to a small value such as .001. Then press the TABLE button (2ND GRAPH), and observe that as x gets close to 0, Y_1 seems to be approaching 1. So the answer is choice (B).

74. If $5x − 8y + 2 = 0$ and $x^2 − 4y = 0$ for $x > 0$, then $x =$

      (A) 2.23
      (B) 2.85
      (C) 3.34
      (D) 4.76
      (E) 5.82

* Algebraic solution: If we add $4y$ to each side of the second equation we get $x^2 = 4y$. If we substitute x^2 for $4y$ into the left hand side of the first equation, we get

$$5x − 8y + 2 = 5x − 2(4y) + 2 = 5x − 2x^2 + 2.$$

So we have $5x − 2x^2 + 2 = 0$ or after multiplying each side of the equation by $−1$ and rearranging terms $2x^2 − 5x − 2 = 0$. We solve for x by using the quadratic formula $x = \frac{-b \pm \sqrt{b^2 - 4ac}}{2a}$.

$$x = \frac{5 \pm \sqrt{(-5)^2 - 4(2)(-2)}}{2(2)} = \frac{5 \pm \sqrt{41}}{4}$$

Since it is given that $x > 0$, we get $x = \frac{5+\sqrt{41}}{4} \approx 2.85$, choice (B).

Notes: (1) There are other ways to solve this probably algebraically. For example, we can multiply the second equation by $−2$ and then add the two equations to get $5x − 2x^2 + 2 = 0$. Now proceed as in the solution above.

(2) This problem can also be solved by plugging in the answer choices. I leave it to the reader to solve the problem this way.

Graphical solution using a TI-84: Press Y=, enter (2 + 5X)/8 for Y_1 and X^2 / 4 for Y_2. Press ZOOM 6 to sketch the graph in a standard window. Now pres CALC (2ND TRACE), select intersect, move the cursor near the positive point of intersection, and press ENTER 3 times. You will see that $x \approx 2.85$, choice (B).

75. If f is a 4th degree polynomial and the points $(1,0)$, $(-3,0)$, $(0,\frac{3}{2})$, and $(2,\frac{175}{6})$ lie on the graph of f, then $f(x)$ could equal

(A) $(x - \frac{3}{2})(x - 1)(x + \frac{1}{3})(x + 3)$

(B) $(x - \frac{3}{2})(x - 1)(x + \frac{1}{3})(x + 2)$

(C) $(x - \frac{3}{2})(x + 1)(x + \frac{1}{3})(x + 3)$

(D) $(x - \frac{3}{2})(x + 1)(x + \frac{1}{3})(x - 3)$

(E) $(x - \frac{1}{3})(x - 1)(x + \frac{3}{2})(x + 3)$

* Since $(1,0)$ and $(-3,0)$ are points on the graph of f, it follows that $x = 1$ and $x = -3$ are zeros of $f(x)$ and so $(x - 1)$ and $(x + 3)$ are both factors of $f(x)$. Only choices A and E have both of these factors, so we can eliminate choices B, C, and D.

We now plug $x = 0$ into choices A and E to get

(A) $(-\frac{3}{2})(-1)(\frac{1}{3})(3) = \frac{3}{2}$

(E) $(-\frac{1}{3})(-1)(\frac{3}{2})(3) = \frac{3}{2}$

Unfortunately, both choices came out correct, so we will have to plug in the last point. We plug $x = 2$ into choices A and E to get

(A) $(2 - \frac{3}{2})(2 - 1)(2 + \frac{1}{3})(2 + 3) = \frac{35}{6}$

(E) $(2 - \frac{1}{3})(2 - 1)(2 + \frac{3}{2})(2 + 3) = \frac{175}{6}$

The answer is choice (E).

Notes: (1) The following are all equivalent for a polynomial $f(x)$:

(a) $(c,0)$ is a point on the graph of $f(x)$.
(b) the point $(c,0)$ is an x-intercept of the graph of $f(x)$.
(c) c is a zero of $f(x)$.
(d) $(x - c)$ is a factor of $f(x)$.

(2) This problem can be solved just by plugging in points. In other words, choices B,C, and D can be eliminated by plugging in the points $(1,0)$ and $(-3,0)$. This method would be more time consuming however.

76. If $g(-x) = -g(x)$ for all real numbers x and if $(2,-6)$ is a point on the graph of g, which of the following points must also be on the graph of $g(x)$?

(A) $(-2,-6)$
(B) $(-2,6)$
(C) $(2, 6)$
(D) $(-6,2)$
(E) $(6,-2)$

* Quick solution: The function $g(x)$ is an odd function. Since the point $(2,-6)$ is on the graph of $g(x)$, so is the point $(-2,6)$, choice (B).

Remarks: (1) See the notes at the end of problem 59 for more about even and odd functions.

(2) The following are equivalent:

(a) $g(x)$ is an odd function.
(b) $g(-x) = -g(x)$ for all x in the domain of g.
(c) The graph of $g(x)$ is symmetrical with respect to the origin.
(d) The point $(-a, -b)$ is on the graph of $g(x)$ whenever the point (a, b) is.
(e) If you rotate the graph of $g(x)$ 180 degrees, the resulting graph is identical to the original.

Alternate solution: Since $(2,-6)$ is on the graph of $g(x)$, we have $g(2) = -6$. So $g(-2) = -g(2) = -(-6) = 6$. Therefore, $(-2,6)$ is on the graph of $g(x)$, choice (B).

Note: $g(a) = b$ is equivalent to "the point (a, b) lies on the graph of g."

LEVEL 3: GEOMETRY

77. Let A and B be points in the plane with $A \neq B$. The set all points in the plane that are closer to B than A is

(A) the interior of a rectangle
(B) the region in the plane bounded by a hyperbola
(C) the region in the plane on one side of a line
(D) the interior of a circle
(E) the exterior of a circle

* A simple drawing shows that the answer is choice (C).

75

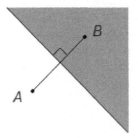

Notes: (1) The set of points at the same distance to A and B is the **perpendicular bisector** of the segment $\overline{AB}$.

(2) The set of all points to the right of (and above) the perpendicular bisector is closer to B than A. This region is shaded in grey in the figure above.

78. If $h: (x, y) \to (x, 3x + y)$ for every pair (x, y) in the plane, for what points (x, y) is it true that $(x, y) \to (x, y)$?

    (A) $(0,0)$ only
    (B) $(0,0)$ and $(0,1)$ only
    (C) The set of points (x, y) such that $y = 0$
    (D) The set of points (x, y) such that $y = 1$
    (E) The set of points (x, y) such that $x = 0$

* **Algebraic solution:** We want to find all points (x, y) such that $x = x$ and $y = 3x + y$. Subtracting y from each side of the second equation yields $0 = 3x$. Dividing this last equation by 3 gives us $0 = x$. So the answer is choice (E).

Remark: This answer can be checked with the following computation $h(0, y) = (0, 3(0) + y) = (0, y)$.

Solution by plugging in a point: Let's try the point $(0,2)$. We have $h(0,2) = (0, 3(0) + 2) = (0,2)$. So we can eliminate choices A, B, C, and D. Therefore, the answer is choice (E).

Note: I used the answer choices as a guide when choosing the point $(0,2)$.

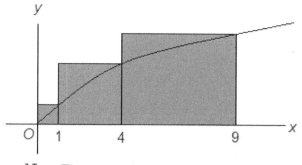

Note: Figure not drawn to scale.

79. The figure above shows a portion of the graph of $y = \sqrt{x}$. What is the sum of the areas of the three circumscribed rectangles shown?

(A) 6
(B) 7
(C) 14
(D) 22
(E) 98

* The leftmost rectangle has a base of 1 and a height of $\sqrt{1} = 1$. So the area of the leftmost rectangle is $1 \cdot 1 = 1$.

The center rectangle has a base of $4 - 1 = 3$ and a height of $\sqrt{4} = 2$. So the area of the center rectangle is $3 \cdot 2 = 6$.

The rightmost rectangle has a base of $9 - 4 = 5$ and a height of $\sqrt{9} = 3$. So the area of the rightmost rectangle is $5 \cdot 3 = 15$.

The sum of these areas is $1 + 6 + 15 = 22$, choice (D).

Notes: (1) The length of the interval $[a, b]$ is $b - a$. For example, the length of $[1,4]$ is $4 - 1 = 3$.

(2) The base of each rectangle is the length of an interval. For example, the base of the center rectangle is the length of $[1,4]$ which is $4 - 1 = 3$.

(3) The height of each rectangle is the y-coordinate of a point on the graph of the function $y = \sqrt{x}$. More specifically, we use the right endpoint of the interval that forms the base of the rectangle. For example, to get the height of the center rectangle we use the right endpoint of the interval $[1,4]$. So the height is $y = \sqrt{4} = 2$.

80. Which of the following could be the coordinates of the center of a circle tangent to the lines $x = 2$ and $y = -1$?

   (A) $(5, -3)$
   (B) $(4, -3)$
   (C) $(3, -3)$
   (D) $(2, -3)$
   (E) $(1, -3)$

Solution by drawing a picture: Let's draw a picture of the two lines.

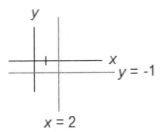

Now note that all of the y-coordinates in the answer choices are -3. So there are two possible circles that will work.

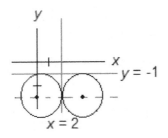

The two circles that would work have centers $(0, -3)$ and $(4, -3)$. So the answer is choice (B).

* **Quick solution:** The y-coordinates in the answer choices are all -3. So the y-coordiante of the center of the circle is two units from the line $y = -1$. Therefore, the x-coordinate of the center must be two units from the line $x = 2$. So the x-coordinate of the center must be 0 or 4, and the answer is choice (B).

81. What is the range of the function defined by

$$h(x) = \begin{cases} \sqrt{x+1}, & x > 5 \\ 7-x, & x \le 5 \end{cases}?$$

(A) All real numbers
(B) All nonnegative real numbers
(C) All positive real numbers
(D) $2 < y < \sqrt{6}$
(E) $y \ge 2$

* **Solution by graphing:** We sketch a graph of the function.

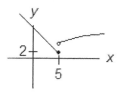

Now note that the minimum y value on the graph is 2, and every y value greater than 2 appears on the graph. So the answer is $y \ge 2$, choice (E).

Notes: (1) The **domain** of the function $f(x)$ is the set of allowed x-values, or equivalently the set of possible inputs of the function. Visually we can see the domain on the graph of the function by looking left to right and omitting any "holes." The domain of the function $h(x)$ above is all real numbers.

(2) The **range** of the function $f(x)$ is the set of possible outputs of the function. More specifically it is the set of all y-values that have the form $f(x)$ for some x in the domain of the function $f(x)$. Visually we can see the range on the graph of the function by looking up and down and omitting any "holes." Note that in the function $h(x)$ above that below $y = 2$ there are no points on the graph, and for every y value greater than or equal to 2 there is at least one point on the graph (in fact, for $y > \sqrt{6}$ there are 2 points on the graph, and for $2 \le y < \sqrt{6}$ there is 1 point on the graph).

(3) You can use your graphing calculator to help you draw this graph. Simply graph each function separately (or at the same time) and then copy the functions onto a single set of axes and restrict them appropriately.

(4) Note that the second piece of the function $h(x)$ is a linear equation with slope $m = -1$ and a y-intercept of $(0,7)$. See problem 18 for more information about lines.

82. A line has parametric equations $x = 3 - t$ and $y = 7 + 2t$, where t is the parameter. The slope of the line is

    (A) –2

    (B) $-\dfrac{1}{2}$

    (C) $\dfrac{3}{7}$

    (D) $\dfrac{7}{3}$

    (E) $\dfrac{7+2t}{3-t}$

Solution using slope-intercept form: We eliminate the parameter. There are several ways to do this algebraically. Let's use the elimination method. We multiply the first equation by 2 and add the 2 equations.

$$2x = 6 - 2t$$
$$\underline{y = 7 + 2t}$$
$$2x + y = 13$$
$$y = -2x + 13$$

We now have an equation of the line in slope-intercept form and we see that the slope is -2, choice (A).

Notes: (1) See the end of problem 18 for more information on slope and slope-intercept form.

(2) There are other ways to eliminate the parameter. For example, we can solve one of the equations for t and then substitute into the other equation (this is the method of substitution). I leave it to the reader to work out the details.

(3) Either of these algebraic procedures can be used to show that the line with parametric equations $x = a + bt$ and $y = c + dt$, where b and d are both nonzero, has slope $\dfrac{d}{b}$. I leave the details to the reader.

* **Quick solution:** By note (3) above, the answer is $\dfrac{2}{-1} = -2$, choice (A).

Vector solution: The given line is parallel to the vector $\langle -1,2 \rangle$. Let's sketch this vector in the plane with initial point at the origin.

80

We see that to get from the point $(-1, 2)$ to the point $(0, 0)$ we must move down 2 and right 1. So the slope is $\frac{-2}{1} = -2$, choice (A).

Note: The line with parametric equations $x = a + bt$ and $y = c + dt$ passes through the point (a, c) and is parallel to the vector $\langle b, d \rangle$.

83. The height of a right circular cylinder is 3 times the diameter of its base. If the volume of the cylinder is 5, what is the radius of the cylinder?

    (A) 0.32
    (B) 0.64
    (C) 0.76
    (D) 0.85
    (E) 1.26

* Algebraic solution: The diameter of a circle is twice the radius. That is $d = 2r$. Since we are given that the height is 3 times the diameter of the base we have $h = 3d = 3(2r) = 6r$. So we have

$$V = \pi r^2 h$$
$$V = \pi r^2 (6r)$$
$$5 = 6\pi r^3$$
$$r^3 = \frac{5}{6\pi}$$
$$r = \sqrt[3]{\frac{5}{6\pi}} \approx 0.64$$

Therefore, the answer is choice (B).

Note: This problem can also be solved by plugging in the answer choices. I leave it to the reader to solve the problem this way.

84. The intersection of a plane with a cone could be which of the following?

    I. A circle
   II. A parabola
  III. A trapezoid

    (A) I only
    (B) II only
    (C) I and II only
    (D) I and III only
    (E) I, II, and III

* Let's look at pictures of the four basic conic sections.

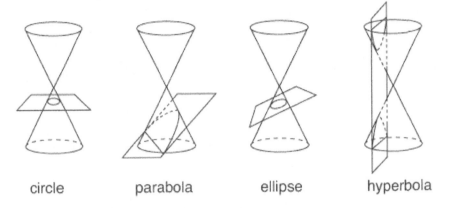

circle   parabola   ellipse   hyperbola

It is now easy to see that the answer is choice (C).

Note: Aside from the four standard conic sections shown in the figure above, there are three additional ways a plane can intersect a cone: a point, a line, and a pair of intersecting lines. These are called the **degenerate cases**. I leave it to the reader to draw pictures of these cases.

LEVEL 3: PROBABILITY AND STATISTICS

85. Of the following lists of numbers, which has the smallest standard deviation?

    (A) 1, 2, 3, 4, 5
    (B) 2, 3, 4, 5, 6
    (C) 1, 3, 5, 7, 9
    (D) 5, 5, 5, 5, 5
    (E) 1, 2, 5, 7, 8

* Quick solution: The standard deviation is a nonnegative number that measures how close the data points are to the arithmetic mean. If the numbers are all the same, then that common number is the mean, and the standard deviation is 0. So the answer is choice (D).

Notes: (1) To actually compute the standard deviation of a list of numbers follow these steps:

a) Find the mean μ of the list of numbers.
b) Subtract each data point from the mean and square the result.
c) Add up all these squares.
d) Divide this result by the number of data points in the list.
e) Take the square root of this last result to get the standard deviation σ.

Let's compute the standard deviation of the list in choice (A) as an example:

a) The mean of the list is $\mu = 3$.
b) We subtract each data point and square to get 4, 1, 0, 1, 4.
c) We add up all these squares to get $4 + 1 + 0 + 1 + 4 = 10$
d) We divide this result by the number of data points: $\frac{10}{5} = 2$.
e) Finally, we take the square root to get $\sigma = \sqrt{2}$.

(2) Standard deviation can be computed easily using a TI-84 calculator. Simply press STAT, select Edit…, enter the data under L1, press STAT again, scroll over to CALC, select 1-Var Stats, and press ENTER.

86. A 7-person committee consisting of 3 men and 4 women is to be chosen from a group of 8 men and 7 women. How many different 7-person committees are possible?

(A) 90
(B) 91
(C) 1240
(D) 1960
(E) 20108

* There are $_8C_3$ ways to choose 3 men from 8, and $_7C_4$ ways to choose 4 women from 7. By the counting principle, the total number of 7-person committees is $_8C_3 \cdot _7C_4 = 1960$.

See problem 53 for more information on the counting principle, and problem 24 for more information on combinations.

87. If $A = \{2, 4, 6, 8, 10\}$, $B = \{-2, 5, 1, -5, k\}$ and $A \cap B = \emptyset$, which of the following CANNOT be the mean of B ?

    (A) 1
    (B) 2
    (C) 3
    (D) 4
    (E) 5

* The sum of the numbers in set B is $-2 + 5 + 1 - 5 + k = k - 1$. Since $A \cap B = \emptyset$, we know that k cannot be 2, 4, 6, 8, or 10. So $k - 1$ cannot be 1, 3, 5, 7, or 9. The sum is $k - 1 = 5$ if and only if the mean of B is $\frac{5}{5} = 1$. So the mean CANNOT be 1, choice (A).

Alternate solution by plugging in answer choices: We can also solve this problem by plugging in answer choices. For example, if we guess that the mean of B is 1, then it follows that the sum of the numbers in B is $1 \cdot 5 = 5$. So $-2 + 5 + 1 - 5 + k = 5$, and therefore $k = 6$. But this contradicts $A \cap B = \emptyset$. So the mean cannot be 1, choice (A).

Notes: (1) In practice it is normally best to start with choice (C) here (as opposed to choice (A)).

(2) To change the mean to a sum we used the formula

Sum = Average · Number

88. In Bakerfield, $\frac{1}{3}$ of the population owns at least 1 cat, $\frac{2}{5}$ of the population owns at least 1 dog, and $\frac{1}{2}$ of the population do not own any pets. What fraction of the population own at least 1 cat and 1 dog?

    (A) $\frac{29}{30}$

    (B) $\frac{1}{2}$

    (C) $\frac{3}{10}$

    (D) $\frac{7}{30}$

    (E) $\frac{1}{5}$

* **Quick computation:** $1 = \frac{1}{3} + \frac{2}{5} - B + \frac{1}{2} = \frac{37}{30} - B$. So $B = \frac{37}{30} - 1 = \frac{7}{30}$, choice (D).

Notes: (1) We used the formula

$$\text{Total} = C + D - B + N$$

where The Total is 1, C is the fraction of the population that have cats, D is the fraction of the population that have dogs, B is the fraction of the population that have both, and N is the fraction of the population that have neither. We are given that $C = \frac{1}{3}$, $D = \frac{2}{5}$, and $N = \frac{1}{2}$.

(2) This problem can also be solved using a Venn Diagram. See problem 54 to see an example of this type of solution.

* Solution by picking a specific value for the Total: If we make the Total 30, then $C = 10$, $D = 12$, and $N = 15$. We can now either use a Venn Diagram or the above formula to get

$$B = C + D + N - \text{Total} = 10 + 12 + 15 - 30 = 7.$$

So the answer is $\frac{7}{30}$, choice (D).

Note: 30 is a good choice to pick for the total because it is the least common denominator of the fractions that appear in the problem.

LEVEL 3: TRIGONOMETRY

89. For $0 < x < \frac{\pi}{2}$,

$$\tan x - \tan(-x) + \sin x - \sin(-x) + \cos x - \cos(-x) =$$

(A) 0
(B) 3
(C) $2 \tan x$
(D) $2 \tan x + 2 \sin x$
(E) $2 \tan x + 2 \sin x + 2 \cos x$

* $\cos x$ is an even function, so that $\cos(-x) = \cos x$. Also, $\sin x$ and $\tan x$ are odd functions, so $\sin(-x) = -\sin x$ and $\tan(-x) = -\tan x$. So we get

$$\tan x - \tan(-x) + \sin x - \sin(-x) + \cos x - \cos(-x)$$
$$= \tan x + \tan x + \sin x + \sin x + \cos x - \cos x$$
$$= 2 \tan x + 2 \sin x$$

85

This is choice (D).

See problem 59 for more about even and odd functions.

Negative Identities: These identities are just restating what was already described above.

$$\cos(-A) = \cos A \qquad\qquad \sin(-A) = -\sin A$$

$$\tan(-A) = -\tan A$$

Note: The reciprocal of an even function is also even, and the reciprocal of an odd function is also odd. So, for example, $\sec x$ is an even function and $\sec(-x) = \sec x$.

90. If $\arctan(\tan x) = \frac{\pi}{4}$ and $-\frac{\pi}{2} < x < \frac{\pi}{2}$, then x could equal

    (A) 0

    (B) $\frac{\pi}{6}$

    (C) $\frac{\pi}{4}$

    (D) $\frac{\pi}{3}$

    (E) $\frac{\pi}{2}$

* **Quick solution:** As long as $-\frac{\pi}{2} < x < \frac{\pi}{2}$, we have $\arctan(\tan x) = x$. So $\arctan(\tan\frac{\pi}{4}) = \frac{\pi}{4}$. Therefore $x = \frac{\pi}{4}$, choice (C).

Notes: (1) Trigonometric functions are usually not invertible. So in order to define the inverse of a trig function, a restriction must first be put on its domain. For example, in order to define $\arctan x$, the inverse of $\tan x$, we must first restrict x to lie strictly between $-\frac{\pi}{2}$ and $\frac{\pi}{2}$.

(2) $\arctan(\tan x) = x$ is true only for $-\frac{\pi}{2} < x < \frac{\pi}{2}$. If x does not satisfy this condition, you should first replace it by an equivalent x value which does satisfy that condition. For example,

$$\arctan(\tan\frac{9\pi}{4}) = \arctan(\tan\frac{\pi}{4}) = \frac{\pi}{4}$$

We can replace $\frac{9\pi}{4}$ by $\frac{\pi}{4}$ because $\frac{9\pi}{4} - 2\pi = \frac{\pi}{4}$. In other words, these are **coterminal** angles. Remember that trig functions have the same value on coterminal angles.

(3) For a less straightforward but similar example, see problem 154.

91. If $\cos x = 0.36$, then $\cos(\pi - x) =$

(A) −0.64
(B) −0.36
(C) 0
(D) 0.36
(E) 0.64

* Calculator solution: $x = \cos^{-1} 0.36,$ so we can simply type

$$\cos(\pi - \cos^{-1} 0.36) \approx -0.36$$

This is choice (B).

Notes: (1) The computation above will only give the correct answer if your calculator is in radian mode.

(2) If your calculator is in degree mode you can get the correct answer by using 180 instead of π.

Solution using an identity: We use the following difference identity:

$$\cos(x - y) = \cos x \cos y + \sin x \sin y$$

$$\cos(\pi - x) = \cos \pi \cos x + \sin \pi \sin x$$

$\cos \pi = -1$ and $\sin \pi = 0$. So $\cos(\pi - x) = -\cos x = -0.36$, choice (B).

92. The polar equation $r \cos \theta = 2$ defines a

(A) point
(B) circle
(C) noncircular ellipse
(D) line
(E) cardioid

* We convert the equation from polar to rectangular. To do this simply recall that $x = r\cos \theta$. So the equation in rectangular is $x = 2$. This is a vertical line. So the answer is choice (D).

Conversion formulas: The following formulas can be used to convert between rectangular and polar coordinates.

$$x = r \cos \theta \qquad y = r \sin \theta$$

$$r^2 = x^2 + y^2 \qquad \tan \theta = \frac{y}{x}$$

The two equations on the first line above are used to convert from polar to rectangular, and the two equations on the second line are used to convert from rectangular to polar.

The following picture shows where these conversion formulas come from:

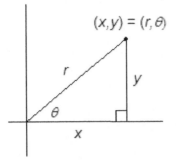

Note, for example, that $\cos \theta = \frac{x}{r}$, so that $x = r\cos \theta$.

The picture above can always be used to convert between rectangular and polar coordinates instead of memorizing the formulas above.

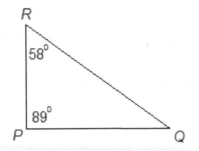

93. In the figure above, if $RQ = 5$, then $PR =$

   (A) 2.72
   (B) 3.02
   (C) 3.76
   (D) 4.02
   (E) 4.24

* **Solution using the Law of Sines:** First note that angle Q has measure $180 - 89 - 58 = 33°$. Let's add this information to the picture.

88

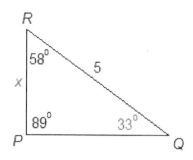

By the Law of Sines we have

$$\frac{\sin 33°}{x} = \frac{\sin 89°}{5}$$

So $x \sin 89° = 5 \sin 33°$ and therefore $x = \dfrac{5 \sin 33°}{\sin 89°} \approx 2.72$, choice (A).

Note: The **Law of Sines** says $\dfrac{\sin A}{a} = \dfrac{\sin B}{b} = \dfrac{\sin C}{c}$ where A, B, and C are the angles in the triangle, and a, b, and c are the lengths of the sides opposite each of these angles.

94.   If $\cos x = k$, then for all x in the interval $0 < x < \frac{\pi}{2}$, $\cot x =$

    (A) $\dfrac{1}{1+k}$

    (B) $\dfrac{k}{\sqrt{1+k^2}}$

    (C) $\dfrac{1}{\sqrt{1+k^2}}$

    (D) $\dfrac{k}{\sqrt{1-k^2}}$

    (E) $\dfrac{1}{\sqrt{1-k^2}}$

* Recall that $\cos x = \dfrac{ADJ}{HYP}$. So we have $k = \dfrac{k}{1} = \dfrac{ADJ}{HYP}$. Let's draw a picture.

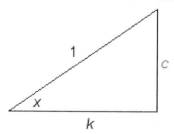

By the Pythagorean Theorem we have $c^2 + k^2 = 1^2$ so that $c^2 = 1 - k^2$ and therefore $c = \sqrt{1 - k^2}$. It follows that

$$\cot x = \frac{\text{ADJ}}{\text{OPP}} = \frac{k}{c} = \frac{k}{\sqrt{1-k^2}}, \text{ choice (D).}$$

Remark: If you do not see why we have $\cos x = \frac{\text{ADJ}}{\text{HYP}}$ or $\cot x = \frac{\text{ADJ}}{\text{OPP}}$ review the basic trigonometry given after the solution to problem 25.

95. $\csc(\sin^{-1} 0.56) =$

     (A) 0.56
     (B) 1.25
     (C) 1.79
     (D) 2.03
     (E) 3.98

* Direct solution: $\csc(\sin^{-1} 0.56) = \dfrac{1}{\sin(\sin^{-1} 0.56)} = \dfrac{1}{0.56} \approx 1.79.$

This is choice (C).

Notes: (1) We have used the reciprocal identity $\csc x = \dfrac{1}{\sin x}$

(2) For a review of the reciprocal identities see problem 29.

(3) There are two different notations used for inverse trig functions. The functions $\arcsin x$ and $\sin^{-1} x$ are two different names for the same function.

(4) $\sin(\sin^{-1} x) = x$ for every x at which $\sin^{-1} x$ is defined. Note however that $\sin^{-1} x$ is only defined for $-1 \le x \le 1$.

(5) Although it is not relevant to this problem you should be aware that $\sin^{-1}(\sin x)$ is **not** always equal to x. See problems 90 and 154 for more information.

96. $\dfrac{\cot x - \csc x \sec x}{\cot x} =$

     (A) $\tan^2 x$
     (B) $-\tan^2 x$
     (C) $\cos^2 x$
     (D) $-\sin^2 x$
     (E) $\sec x \tan x$

* Solution using trig identities:

$$\frac{\cot x - \csc x \sec x}{\cot x} = \frac{\frac{\cos x}{\sin x} - \frac{1}{\sin x}\frac{1}{\cos x}}{\frac{\cos x}{\sin x}} = \frac{\cos^2 x - 1}{\cos^2 x}$$

$$= \frac{\cos^2 x}{\cos^2 x} - \frac{1}{\cos^2 x} = 1 - \sec^2 x = -\tan^2 x$$

This is choice (B).

Notes: (1) We get the first equation by using the quotient identity $\cot x = \frac{\cos x}{\sin x}$ and the reciprocal identities $\csc x = \frac{1}{\sin x}$ and $\sec x = \frac{1}{\cos x}$.

(2) The second expression is a complex fraction. We simplify this complex fraction by multiplying the numerator and denominator by $\sin x \cos x$. We chose this expression because it is the least common denominator of the three simple fractions within the complex fraction.

(3) See problem 63 to see why $1 + \tan^2 x = \sec^2 x$. From this we get that $\sec^2 x - 1 = \tan^2 x$. Therefore $1 - \sec^2 x = -(\sec^2 x - 1) = -\tan^2 x$.

(4) This problem can also be solved by picking a value for x. I leave the details to the reader.

LEVEL 4: NUMBER THEORY

97. Under which of the following conditions can $\frac{x+y}{xy^2}$ be negative?

    (A) $0 < x < y$
    (B) $x < 0 < y$
    (C) $x < y < 0$
    (D) $y < x < 0$
    (E) None of the above

* If x and y are both positive, then $x + y$ is positive and xy^2 is positive. Therefore, we can eliminate choice A. Furthermore, since B, C, and D all have $x < 0$, we will assume that x is negative. It follows that the denominator is negative, and therefore the numerator must be positive. Since x is negative, in order for $x + y$ to be positive, y must be positive. Based on these guidelines let's try $x = -1$ and $y = 3$. We then have.

$$\frac{x+y}{xy^2} = \frac{-1+3}{(-1)(3^2)} = \frac{2}{-9} = -\frac{9}{2}.$$

Once again note that $x < 0 < y$, choice (B).

Remarks: (1) Since y^2 is always nonnegative we can disregard it and just look at the expression $\frac{x+y}{x}$.

(2) We could have also argued that if x and y are both negative, then the numerator and denominator are negative, making the fraction positive. This allows to eliminate choices C and D. Now we simply have to find suitable x and y satisfying the condition in choice B.

(3) We can start plugging in numbers for x and y right away without using any reasoning. But guessing blindly like this could be a bit time consuming.

98. $\dfrac{[n!]^3}{[(n+1)!]^3} =$

   (A) $\dfrac{1}{n+1}$

   (B) $\dfrac{1}{n^2+2n+1}$

   (C) $\dfrac{1}{n^3+3n^2+3n+1}$

   (D) $\dfrac{n}{n+1}$

   (E) n^3

* Algebraic solution: $\dfrac{[n!]^3}{[(n+1)!]^3} = \dfrac{[n!]^3}{(n+1)^3[n!]^3} = \dfrac{1}{(n+1)^3} = \dfrac{1}{n^3+3n^2+3n+1}$, choice (C).

Notes: (1) Observe that $(n + 1)! = (n + 1)n!$.

For example, $5! = 5 \cdot 4 \cdot 3 \cdot 2 \cdot 1 = 5 \cdot 4!$.

In fact, we can pull out as many factors as we like. So we also have that $5! = 5 \cdot 4 \cdot 3! = 20 \cdot 3!$, and so on.

(2) Using (1) we have that $[(n + 1)!]^3 = [(n + 1)n!]^3 = (n + 1)^3[n!]^3$.

(3) We can compute $(n + 1)^3$ in several different ways. The quickest is to use the **binomial theorem** which says that

$$(x + y)^n = {}_nC_0x^ny^0 + {}_nC_1x^{n-1}y^1 + \cdots + {}_nC_nx^0y^n$$

So we have

$$(n + 1)^3 = {}_3C_0n^31^0 + {}_3C_1n^21^1 + {}_3C_2n^11^2 + {}_3C_3n^01^3$$
$$= n^3 + 3n^2 + 3n + 1$$

An alternative is to write

$$(n + 1)^3 = (n + 1)(n + 1)(n + 1) = (n^2 + 2n + 1)(n + 1).$$

We can multiply these last two factors using the method given in problem 9 to get

$$n^3 + 3n^2 + 3n + 1$$

(4) This problem can also be solved by picking numbers. For example, try letting $n = 3$. Then $\frac{[n!]^3}{[(n+1)!]^3} = \frac{1}{64}$, and we can eliminate all answer choices except choice C. I leave the details of this method to the reader.

99. If the 50th term of an arithmetic sequence is 125 and the 75th term of the sequence is 300, what is the first term of the sequence?

   (A) –220
   (B) –218
   (C) 0
   (D) 218
   (E) 220

* Quick solution: We can find the common difference of this arithmetic sequence with the computation

$$d = \frac{300-125}{75-50} = \frac{175}{25} = 7.$$

The first term is $125 - 49(7) = -218$, choice (B).

Remark: See problem 3 for more information about arithmetic sequences and for more ways to solve this problem.

100. If x is a real number such that $\sqrt{x^2} = -x$, then x must be

   (A) positive
   (B) negative
   (C) nonpositive
   (D) nonnegative
   (E) 0

Solution by picking numbers: If $x = 0$, then

$$\sqrt{x^2} = \sqrt{0^2} = 0 = -0 = -x.$$

So $x = 0$ satisfies the given condition. We can therefore eliminate choices A and B.

93

If $x = -4$, then

$$\sqrt{x^2} = \sqrt{(-4)^2} = \sqrt{16} = 4 = -(-4) = -x.$$

So $x = -4$ satisfies the given condition. We can therefore eliminate D and E. So the answer is choice (C).

* Quick solution: $\sqrt{x^2} = |x|$ which is equal to $-x$ if x nonpositive.

Notes: (1) Here are some basic definitions for your review:

x is positive if and only if $x > 0$
x is negative if and only if $x < 0$
x is nonpositive if and only if $x \leq 0$
x is nonnegative if and only if $x \geq 0$

(2) $|x|$ is usually defined to be x if $x \geq 0$ and $-x$ if $x < 0$. Note however, that if $x = 0$, then $x = -x$. So the definition *could* be stated so that $|x|$ is $-x$ if $x \leq 0$.

LEVEL 4: ALGEBRA AND FUNCTIONS

101. Suppose the graph of $g(x) = -2x^3$ is translated 2 units down and 3 units left. If the resulting graph represents $G(x)$, what is the value of $G(-.5)$?

   (A) -33.25
   (B) -28.75
   (C) -17.25
   (D) -11.5
   (E) -2.25

* $G(x) = -2(x + 3)^3 - 2$. So $G(-.5) = -2(-.5 + 3)^3 - 2 = -33.25$.

This is choice (A).

Notes: (1) To translate the graph of a function down 2 units we subtract 2 from the original function.

(2) To translate the graph of a function left 3 units we replace x by $x + 3$ in the original function.

Review of basic transformations: Let $y = f(x)$, and $k > 0$. We can move the graph of f around by applying the following basic transformations.

$y = f(x) + k$ shift up k units
$y = f(x) - k$ shift down k units
$y = f(x - k)$ shift right k units
$y = f(x + k)$ shift left k units
$y = -f(x)$ reflect in x-axis
$y = f(-x)$ reflect in y-axis.

102. If $a(x) = \sqrt[5]{x^3 - 2}$, what is $a^{-1}(2.2)$?

    (A) 3.77
    (B) 4.23
    (C) 4.87
    (D) 5.01
    (E) 5.76

* Solution by starting with choice (C): We are looking for a value of x so that $a(x) = 2.2$. Let's start with choice (C) and guess that $x = 4.87$. We have $a(4.87) = \sqrt[5]{4.87^3 - 2} \approx 2.6$. This is too big so we can eliminate choices C, D, and E.

Let's try choice (A) next and guess that $x = 3.77$. We have that $a(3.77) = \sqrt[5]{3.77^3 - 2} \approx 2.2$. So the answer is choice (A).

Solution by finding the inverse function: We interchange the roles of x and y and solve for y.

$$a(x) = \sqrt[5]{x^3 - 2}$$
$$y = \sqrt[5]{x^3 - 2}$$
$$x = \sqrt[5]{y^3 - 2}$$
$$x^5 = y^3 - 2$$
$$x^5 + 2 = y^3$$
$$\sqrt[3]{x^5 + 2} = y$$
$$a^{-1}(x) = \sqrt[3]{x^5 + 2}$$

So $a^{-1}(2.2) = \sqrt[3]{2.2^5 + 2} \approx 3.77$, choice (A).

103. The formula $A = P(1.025)^{2t}$ gives the amount A that an account will be worth after an initial investment P is compounded twice a year at an annual rate of 5% for t years. How many years will it take an initial investment to triple?

(A) 9.3
(B) 18.6
(C) 21.2
(D) 22.2
(E) 24.7

* **Algebraic solution:** Since the initial investment is P and we want the initial investment to triple, we replace A by $3P$ and solve for t.

$$3P = P(1.025)^{2t}$$
$$3 = (1.025)^{2t}$$
$$\ln 3 = \ln(1.025)^{2t}$$
$$\ln 3 = 2t \ln(1.025)$$
$$\frac{\ln 3}{2\ln(1.025)} = t$$

So $t = \dfrac{\ln 3}{2\ln(1.025)} \approx 22.2$, choice (D).

Remark: (1) See the end of problem 4 for the basic laws of logarithms.

(2) When solving an equation for a variable that is in an exponent, take the natural logarithm of each side of the equation and bring the exponent down in front of the logarithm. This was done in going from the second equation to the third equation, and from the third equation to the fourth equation above.

104. If $(2.47)^a(2.47)^b = (1.23)^b$, what is the value of $\dfrac{a}{b}$?

(A) –0.91
(B) –0.77
(C) –0.50
(D) 0.23
(E) 0.49

* Let's begin by dividing each side of the given equation by $(2.47)^b$:

$$(2.47)^a = \left(\frac{1.23}{2.47}\right)^b$$

96

Now let's take the natural logarithm of each side.

$$\ln(2.47)^a = \ln\left(\frac{1.23}{2.47}\right)^b$$

We can now use a basic property of logarithms to bring the exponents out in front.

$$a\ln(2.47) = b\ln\left(\frac{1.23}{2.47}\right)$$

Finally, we perform cross division to bring b to the left and $\ln(2.47)$ to the right.

$$\frac{a}{b} = \frac{\ln\left(\frac{1.23}{2.47}\right)}{\ln(2.47)} \approx -.77$$

This is choice (B).

Remarks: (1) See the end of problem 4 for the basic laws of logarithms.

(2) We can also begin this problem by rewriting the left hand side as $(2.47)^{a+b}$ and then taking the natural logarithm of each side. I leave it to the reader to work out the details.

105. If $\begin{vmatrix} a & b & c \\ d & e & f \\ g & h & i \end{vmatrix} = k$, then $\begin{vmatrix} 2a & 2b & 2c \\ 2d & 2e & 2f \\ 2g & 2h & 2i \end{vmatrix} =$

    (A) $2k$
    (B) $4k$
    (C) $8k$
    (D) $16k$
    (E) $512k$

* $\begin{vmatrix} 2a & 2b & 2c \\ 2d & 2e & 2f \\ 2g & 2h & 2i \end{vmatrix} = 2^3 \begin{vmatrix} a & b & c \\ d & e & f \\ g & h & i \end{vmatrix} = 8k$, choice (C).

Notes: (1) If A is a matrix, then $|A|$ is called the **determinant** of A.

(2) We do not need to know how to compute a determinant to solve this problem. We only need to understand a single property of determinants.

(3) If A and B are matrices and B has all the same entries as matrix A except that all the entries in a single row of B are equal to the entries in the corresponding row of A multiplied by c, then $|B| = c|A|$.

For example, $\begin{vmatrix} 3 & 4 \\ 1 & 2 \end{vmatrix} = 2$. Therefore, $\begin{vmatrix} 3 & 4 \\ 5 & 10 \end{vmatrix} = 5 \begin{vmatrix} 3 & 4 \\ 1 & 2 \end{vmatrix} = 5 \cdot 2 = 10$.

(4) Observe that if you want to use the above property to pull out a number from more than 1 row, you need to do one row at a time.

For example, $\begin{vmatrix} 15 & 20 \\ 5 & 10 \end{vmatrix} = 5 \begin{vmatrix} 3 & 4 \\ 5 & 10 \end{vmatrix} = 5 \cdot 5 \begin{vmatrix} 3 & 4 \\ 1 & 2 \end{vmatrix} = 5^2 \cdot 2 = 50$.

(5) If we want to pull out the same number c from all rows simultaneously, we get $|B| = c^n|A|$ where A and B are $n \times n$ matrices.

For example, $\begin{vmatrix} 15 & 20 \\ 5 & 10 \end{vmatrix} = 5^2 \begin{vmatrix} 3 & 4 \\ 1 & 2 \end{vmatrix} = 5^2 \cdot 2 = 50$.

(6) Since the matrix given in this problem is 3×3, the exponent we needed to use when pulling out a 2 from all 3 rows simultaneously was 3.

(7) This isn't needed for this problem, but in general $\begin{vmatrix} a & b \\ c & d \end{vmatrix} = ad - bc$.

For example, $\begin{vmatrix} 3 & 4 \\ 1 & 2 \end{vmatrix} = 3 \cdot 2 - 4 \cdot 1 = 6 - 4 = 2$.

106. The graph of the function $f(x) = -3x^2 + 2x - k$ is tangent to the x-axis. What is the value of k ?

(A) $\frac{1}{4}$

(B) $\frac{1}{3}$

(C) $\frac{1}{2}$

(D) 1

(E) 2

* **Solution using general form for a quadratic equation:** The x-coordinate of the vertex of the graph is $-\dfrac{b}{2a} = -\dfrac{2}{2(-3)} = \dfrac{1}{3}$. So the point $\left(\frac{1}{3}, 0\right)$ is on the graph of the function. Therefore,

$$0 = -3\left(\tfrac{1}{3}\right)^2 + 2\left(\tfrac{1}{3}\right) - k = -\tfrac{1}{3} + \tfrac{2}{3} - k = \tfrac{1}{3} - k.$$

So $k = \dfrac{1}{3}$, choice (B).

Notes: (1) The general form for a quadratic function is

$$y = ax^2 + bx + c.$$

The graph of this function is a parabola whose vertex has x-coordinate

$$-\frac{b}{2a}$$

The parabola opens upwards if $a > 0$ and downwards if $a < 0$.

(2) The vertex of the parabola in this problem lies on the x-axis because the parabola is given to be tangent to the x-axis. So the y-coordinate of the vertex is 0.

Solution using the discriminant: Since the graph of this quadratic function is tangent to the x-axis, the discriminant of the function is zero.

$$b^2 - 4ac = 0$$
$$2^2 - 4(-3)(-k) = 0$$
$$4 - 12k = 0$$
$$4 = 12k$$
$$k = \frac{4}{12} = \frac{1}{3}$$

This is choice (B).

Notes: (1) Recall the quadratic formula: If $ax^2 + bx + c = 0$, then

$$x = \frac{-b \pm \sqrt{b^2 - 4ac}}{2a}$$

The expression under the square root $b^2 - 4ac$ is called the **discriminant**

(2) If the discriminant is positive, then the quadratic function has 2 distinct real roots, and the graph of the function passes through the x-axis.

(3) If the discriminant is negative, then the quadratic function has 2 complex roots, and the graph of the function does not touch the x-axis.

(4) If the discriminant is zero, then the quadratic function has 1 real root, and the graph of the function is tangent to the x-axis.

107. $|-10 + 24i| =$

    (A) –34
    (B) 34i
    (C) 34
    (D) 26i
    (E) 26

Direct solution: $|-10 + 24i| = \sqrt{(-10)^2 + (24)^2} = 26$, choice (E).

Notes: (1) The **absolute value** of the complex number $a + bi$ is

$$|a + bi| = \sqrt{a^2 + b^2}.$$

(2) The complex number $a + bi$ can be plotted as the point (a, b) in the complex plane. Geometrically, $|a + bi|$ is the distance from the origin to this point.

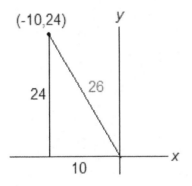

* **Quick solution:** Since $10 = 2(5)$ and $24 = 2(12)$, we have that $|-10 + 24i| = 2(13) = 26$.

Notes: (1) We used the Pythagorean triple 5, 12, 13 here. We doubled each of these numbers to get the triple 10, 24, 26.

(2) If you do not remember the appropriate Pythagorean triple, you can use the Pythagorean Theorem instead.

(3) See problem 47 for more information on Pythagorean triples and the Pythagorean Theorem.

100

108. If $g(x, y) = g(-x, -y)$ for all real numbers x and y, then g can be which of the following functions ?

    (A) $x + y$
    (B) $x^2 + y$
    (C) $x^3 + y^2$
    (D) $\frac{x+y}{x-y}$
    (E) $\frac{x^2+y^2}{x-y}$

* **Solution by starting with choice (C):** Let's start with choice (C) and guess that $g(x, y) = x^3 + y^2$. Then

$$g(-x, -y) = (-x)^3 + (-y)^2 = -x^3 + y^2 \neq g(x, y).$$

So we can eliminate choice (C).

Let's try choice (D) next and guess that that $g(x, y) = \frac{x+y}{x-y}$. Then

$$g(-x, -y) = \frac{-x-y}{-x-(-y)} = \frac{-(x+y)}{-(x-y)} = \frac{x+y}{x-y} = g(x, y).$$

So the answer is choice (D).

Notes: (1) This problem can also be solved by picking numbers. I leave the details to the reader.

(2) It is easy to eliminate choices A, B, and C right away. These three choices are polynomials, and each one has at least one odd power of x or y. Note that x can be written as x^1, and therefore is an odd power of x.

LEVEL 4: GEOMETRY

109. Suppose that $\triangle ABC$ is not isosceles and altitude $\overline{BD}$ is drawn. An indirect proof of the statement "$\overline{BD}$ does <u>not</u> bisect $\overline{AC}$" could begin with the assumption that

    (A) $\triangle ABC$ is not isosceles
    (B) $\triangle ABC$ is isosceles
    (C) $\overline{BD}$ is not an altitude
    (D) $\overline{BD}$ does not bisect $\overline{AC}$
    (E) $\overline{BD}$ bisects $\overline{AC}$

* To prove a statement indirectly we begin with the negation of the conclusion. In this problem the conclusion is "$\overline{BD}$ does <u>not</u> bisect $\overline{AC}$." So to prove this statement indirectly we begin with "$\overline{BD}$ bisects $\overline{AC}$," choice (E).

Notes: (1) This is really a Logic problem, and not a Geometry problem.

(2) A statement of the form "if p, then q" is known as a **conditional** statement. An example of such a statement is "If you are a cat, then you have fur." Another common way to say this is "All cats have fur."

There are 3 other statements that often come up in association with a conditional statement. Let's use the example above to illustrate.

Conditional: If you are a cat, then you have fur.
Converse: If you have fur, then you are a cat.
Inverse: If you are not a cat, then you do not have fur.
Contrapositive: If you do not have fur, then you are not a cat.

The most important thing to know for this test is that the contrapositive is logically equivalent to the original conditional statement! The converse and inverse are not.

For example, suppose the conditional statement "All cats have fur" is true. You may want to rewrite this as "If you are a cat, then you have fur." It follows that "If you do not have fur, then you are not a cat" is also true.

In particular, if you are given the statement "Skittles does not have fur," you can infer "Skittles is not a cat."

Note that neither the converse nor the inverse is logically equivalent to the original conditional statement, but they are equivalent to each other.

(3) There are two types of proofs that can be classified as **indirect.** The first is a **proof by contrapositive**. The second is a **proof by contradiction**.

(4) Let's assume we want to prove the conditional statement "if p, then q." In a **direct proof** we would assume that p is true, and use this to argue that q is true. In a proof by contrapositive we would assume that q is false and use this to argue that p is false. In a proof by contradiction we would assume that p is true and q is false, and then produce a contradiction (this is a statement we know to be false).

(5) The given problem can be formulated as "if $\triangle ABC$ is not isosceles, then $\overline{BD}$ does not bisect $\overline{AC}$." A proof by contrapositive would start with "$\overline{BD}$ bisects $\overline{AC}$," whereas a proof by contradiction would start with "$\triangle ABC$ is not isosceles and $\overline{BD}$ bisects $\overline{AC}$."

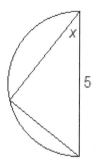

110. The figure above shows a triangle inscribed in a semicircle. What is the area of the triangle in terms of x?

    (A) $5\sin x$

    (B) $5\cos x$

    (C) $5\tan x$

    (D) $\dfrac{25}{2}\sin x \cos x$

    (E) $25\sin x \tan x$

* Note that the angle opposite the side of length 5 is an inscribed angle intercepting an arc of 180°. Therefore, it is a right angle. Let's label the two sides a and b.

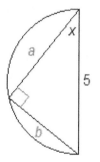

$\cos x = \dfrac{\text{ADJ}}{\text{HYP}} = \dfrac{a}{5}$. So $a = 5\cos x$. Similarly, $\sin x = \dfrac{\text{OPP}}{\text{HYP}} = \dfrac{b}{5}$. So $b = 5\sin x$. So the area of the triangle is $\dfrac{1}{2}ab = \dfrac{1}{2}(5\cos x)(5\sin x) = \dfrac{25}{2}\cos x \sin x$, choice (D).

See problem 25 for an extensive review of basic trigonometry.

103

111. If the complex number z is plotted as a point in the complex plane, it appears in the third quadrant. In which quadrant does $-iz$ lie?

(A) I
(B) II
(C) III
(D) IV
(E) Cannot be determined from the given information

* **Quick solution:** The transformation $z \to iz$ is a 90° rotation counterclockwise and the transformation $z \to -iz$ is a 90° rotation clockwise. Since z is in the third quadrant, $-iz$ must be in the second quadrant, choice (B).

Remark: Here is a picture.

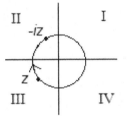

Solution by picking a point: Let's choose a complex number in the third quadrant such as $z = -3 - 2i$. Then

$$-iz = -i(-3 - 2i) = 3i + 2i^2 = 3i - 2 = -2 + 3i.$$

$-2 + 3i$ is in the second quadrant, so a good guess is choice (B). A few moment's thought should convince you that it doesn't matter which third quadrant point was chosen. So the answer is choice (B).

Note: $i = \sqrt{-1}$ is the **imaginary unit**. It follows that $i^2 = -1$.

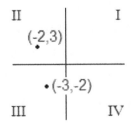

Solution using an arbitrary third quadrant complex number: Let a and b be arbitrary positive real numbers. A complex number in the third quadrant has the form $z = -a - bi$. It follows that

$$-iz = -i(-a - bi) = ai + bi^2 = ai - b = -b + ai$$

This number is in the second quadrant. So the answer is choice (B).

112. A cube with volume 64 cubic inches is inscribed in a sphere so that each vertex of the cube touches the sphere. What is the length of the radius, in inches, of the sphere?

(A) 1.23
(B) 3
(C) 3.46
(D) 6.92
(E) 12

* The diameter of the sphere is the long diagonal of the cube.

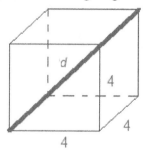

Since the volume of the cube is 64, the length of a side of the cube is 4 (we get this by taking the cube root of 64). Thus, the diameter of the sphere is given by $d^2 = a^2 + b^2 + c^2 = 16 + 16 + 16 = 48$.

So $d = \sqrt{48}$ and the radius is $r = \dfrac{d}{2} = \dfrac{\sqrt{48}}{2} \approx 3.46$, choice (C).

113. What is the length of the major axis of the ellipse whose equation is $50x^2 + 40y^2 = 180$?

(A) 2.12
(B) 3.79
(C) 4.24
(D) 8.49
(E) 9

* We put the ellipse into standard form by dividing each side of the equation by 180 to get $\frac{x^2}{3.6} + \frac{y^2}{4.5} = 1$. So we have $a^2 = 3.6$ and $b^2 = 4.5$. Since b^2 is larger, the length of the major axis is $2b = 2\sqrt{4.5} \approx 4.24$, choice (C).

Notes: See problem 19 for information about ellipses.

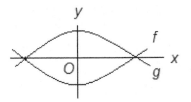

114. Portions of the graphs of f and g are shown above. Which of the following could be a portion of the graph of fg ?

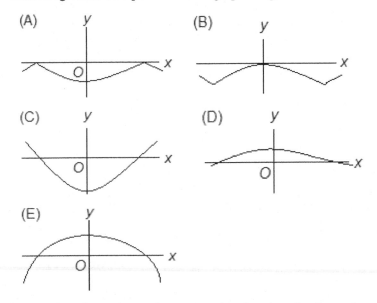

* Since the two functions always have opposite sign (one is above the x-axis, the other below), the product must always be negative (except where it is zero). So the graph of fg lies entirely below the x-axis, with the exception of the two zeros. So we can eliminate choices C, D, and E. Choice B does not have the zeros in the right place, so the answer is choice (A).

115. If $g(x) = \frac{2}{3}x^3 - \frac{1}{2}x^2 - 10x + 2$, which of the following statements are true?

> I. g is decreasing for $x > -2$.
> II. g is increasing for $x < -2$.
> III. $g(x) \geq -11$ for all $x \geq 0$.

   (A) I only
   (B) II only
   (C) III only
   (D) I and II only
   (E) II and III only

* **Solution by graphing:** We enter the function into our TI-84 calculator and press ZOOM 6 to view the graph in a standard window. We then use the WINDOW button and adjust Ymin and Ymax to about -20 and 20, respectively (this is to ensure that the relative maximum and minimum appear in the viewing window). Using the maximum feature under CALC we find that there is a relative maximum at $x = -2$. So II is true. III is false however: although the function begins decreasing at $x = -2$, we can see from the graph that it begins to increase a bit later. Finally, we can use the TRACE feature, or find the relative minimum to see that there are positive values of x for which $g(x) < -11$. So the answer is choice (B).

Notes: (1) See problem 74 to see how to enter functions for graphing more explicitly. The maximum and minimum features can be used just like the intersect feature was used as described problem 74.

(2) The maximum and minimum in this problem are not **absolute** maxima and minima because they are not the highest and lowest points on the graph. They are only higher and lower than all points **near** them. This is why we call them **relative** maximum and minimum.

(3) This problem can also be solved using calculus. A full calculus solution is a bit beyond the scope of this book, but students with some calculus experience can take the derivative and set it to zero to find the critical numbers, and use the first derivative test to find where the function is increasing and decreasing.

107

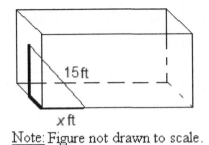

x ft

Note: Figure not drawn to scale.

116. A rectangular room measures 20 feet in length and width and 10 feet in height. A fly, with a broken wing, rests at a point 3 feet down from the ceiling at the middle of one end. Some food is located on the floor at a straight line distance of 15 feet from the fly along the edge of the room. The fly walks straight down to the floor, then along the edges of the room straight to the food as shown in the figure above. What is the value of x?

(A) 4.23
(B) 8.72
(C) 10.77
(D) 13.27
(E) 73.7

* We use the Generalized Pythagorean Theorem to get

$$15^2 = x^2 + 10^2 + 7^2$$
$$225 = x^2 + 149$$
$$x^2 = 225 - 149 = 76$$
$$x = \sqrt{76} \approx 8.72.$$

This is choice (B).

Notes: (1) The **Generalized Pythagorean Theorem** says that the length d of the long diagonal of a rectangular solid is given by

$$d^2 = a^2 + b^2 + c^2$$

where a, b and c are the length, width and height of the rectangular solid.

(2) Since the width of the room is 20 feet, the unlabeled horizontal bold line segment has length 10 feet.

(3) Since the height of the room is 10 feet and the fly is 3 feet down from the ceiling, the vertical bold line segment has length $10 - 3 = 7$ feet.

LEVEL 4: PROBABILITY AND STATISTICS

117. In how many ways can 8 books be split into two piles, one with 5 books and the other with 3 books?

    (A) 48
    (B) 52
    (C) 56
    (D) 3136
    (E) 6720

* We simply need to count the number of ways to choose 5 books from 8. This is $_8C_5 = 56$, choice (C).

Notes: (1) See problem 24 for more information on combinations.

(2) Once we choose 5 books from the 8, this automatically also chooses the other pile of 3. A common mistake would be to also compute $_8C_3$ and multiply the two numbers together (this is choice D).

(3) We could also compute $_8C_3$ instead. In other words, we can count the number of ways to choose 3 books from the 8. In this case the pile of 5 will automatically be determined.

(4) Note that in general $_nC_r = {_nC_{n-r}}$. For example, $_8C_5 = {_8C_3}$.

118. Billy has an 8% chance of shooting a basket from the foul line. If Billy makes 3 attempts to make a basket from the foul line, what is the probability that he makes at least 2 shots?

    (A) 0.0005
    (B) 0.0177
    (C) 0.0182
    (D) 0.1817
    (E) 0.9818

* **Solution using the binomial probability formula:** The probability of an event with probability p occurring exactly r out of n times is

$$_nC_r \cdot p^r \cdot (1-p)^{n-r}$$

In this question, $n = 3$, $p = 0.08$ and r can be 2 **or** 3. So the desired probability is

$$_3C_2 \cdot (0.08)^2 \cdot (0.92)^1 + {_3C_3} \cdot (0.08)^3 \cdot (0.92)^0 \approx 0.0182$$

This is choice (C).

Note: "At least 2 shots" means "2 shots or 3 shots." This is why we have to use the binomial probability formula twice: once for $r = 2$ and once for $r = 3$. We then add the two results.

$$S = 25.33H + 353.16$$

119. The linear regression model above is based on an analysis of the relationship between SAT math scores (S) and the number of hours spent studying for SAT math (H). Based on this model, which of the following statements must be true?

   I. The slope indicates that as H increases by 1, S decreases by 25.33.
   II. For a student that studies 15 hours for SAT math, the predicted SAT math score is greater than 700.
   III. There is a negative correlation between H and S.

   (A) I only
   (B) II only
   (C) III only
   (D) I and II only
   (E) II and III only

* The slope of the line is $25.33 = \frac{25.33}{1}$. This indicates that as H increases by 1, S increases by 25.33. Also since the slope is positive, there is a **positive correlation** between H and S. So I and III are false, and the answer must be choice (B).

Notes: (1) We did not have to check II because once we determined that I and III were false, there was only one answer choice left that excluded both of them.

(2) For completeness let's check that II is true. To see this, we just need to perform the following: $25.33(15) + 353.16 = 733.11 > 700$.

120. A group of students take a test and the average score is 65. One more student takes the test and receives a score of 92 increasing the average score of the group to 68. How many students were in the initial group?

    (A) 5
    (B) 6
    (C) 7
    (D) 8
    (E) 9

* **Solution by changing averages to sums:** Let n be the number of students in the initial group. We change the average to a sum using the formula

Sum = Average · Number

So the initial **Sum** is $65n$.

When we take into account the new student, we can find the new sum in two different ways.

(1) We can add the new score to the old sum to get $65n + 92$.

(2) We can compute the new sum directly using the simple formula above to get $68(n + 1) = 68n + 68$.

We now set these equal to each other and solve for n:

$$65n + 92 = 68n + 68$$
$$24 = 3n$$
$$n = 8.$$

This is choice (D).

LEVEL 4: TRIGONOMETRY

121. If $180° < \theta < 270°$ and $\cot \theta = 10$, then $\sec \theta =$

    (A) -1.005
    (B) -0.995
    (C) 0.213
    (D) 0.995
    (E) 1.005

* Calculator solution: Since $\cot\theta = 10$, $\tan\theta = \frac{1}{10}$. So we have that $\theta = 180 + \tan^{-1}\frac{1}{10} \approx 185.711$ So $\cos\theta \approx \cos 185.711 \approx -.995$. Finally, $\sec\theta = \frac{1}{\cos\theta} \approx \frac{1}{-.995} \approx -1.005$, choice (A).

Notes: (1) Make sure your calculator is in degree mode for this problem.

(2) Recall that cotangent is the reciprocal of tangent. So $\tan\theta = \frac{1}{\cot\theta}$.

(3) Recall that secant is the reciprocal of cosine. So $\sec\theta = \frac{1}{\cos\theta}$.

(4) See problem 25 for a more extensive review of basic trigonometry.

(5) When we compute $\tan^{-1}\frac{1}{10}$ in our calculator we always get a first quadrant angle. Since the problem says $180° < \theta < 270°$ we need to compute the corresponding third quadrant angle. We get this angle by adding $180°$ to $\tan^{-1}\frac{1}{10}$.

Solution by drawing a picture:

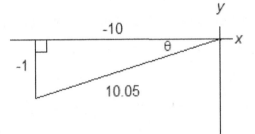

Since $180° < \theta < 270°$ we draw a right triangle in the third quadrant.

Next, since $\cot\theta = 10 = \frac{10}{1}$, and $\cot\theta = \frac{\text{ADJ}}{\text{OPP}}$, we label the adjacent side to θ with 10 and the opposite side with 1. Note that we also attached minus signs to these numbers because we are moving left and down (the signs are optional – see the note below). We use the Pythagorean Theorem to get the hypotenuse: $\sqrt{10^2 + 1^2} = \sqrt{101} \approx 10.05$. We ALWAYS make the hypotenuse positive.

Finally, we have $\sec\theta = \frac{\text{HYP}}{\text{ADJ}} = \frac{10.05}{-10} = -1.005$, choice (A).

Note: As an alternative, we can leave the minus signs out, and after we finish the computation just remember that secant is negative in the third quadrant. You may want to go back and look at the picture in problem 61. Also remember that secant is the reciprocal of cosine. Therefore, for a specific angle, secant and cosine always have the same sign.

122. What is the period of the graph of $= \frac{2}{3}\tan(\frac{5}{2}\pi\theta - 2)$?

    (A) $\frac{4}{15}$

    (B) $\frac{2}{5}$

    (C) $\frac{2}{3}$

    (D) $\frac{4\pi}{15}$

    (E) $\frac{2\pi}{5}$

* The period of the graph of $y = a\tan(bx - c)$ is $\frac{\pi}{b}$. So the period of the graph of the given function is $\frac{\pi}{\frac{5\pi}{2}} = \pi \div \frac{5\pi}{2} = \pi \cdot \frac{2}{5\pi} = \frac{2}{5}$, choice (B).

123. Points P and Q lie on a circle of radius 8 with center O. If the measure of $\angle OPQ$ is 50°, what is the length of chord $\overline{PQ}$?

    (A) 10.0
    (B) 10.1
    (C) 10.2
    (D) 10.3
    (E) 10.4

* Let's draw a picture.

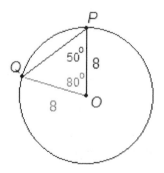

By drawing in segment $\overline{OQ}$ we get an isosceles triangle. Since $\angle OPQ$ has measure 50°, so does $\angle OQP$, and it follows that $\angle POQ$ has measure $180 - 50 - 50 = 80°$. We can now use the Law of Sines to find PQ.

$$\frac{\sin 80°}{PQ} = \frac{\sin 50°}{8}$$

So $PQ \sin 50° = 8\sin 80°$, and $PQ = \dfrac{8 \sin 80°}{\sin 50°} \approx 10.3$, choice (D).

Note: The **Law of Sines** says $\dfrac{\sin A}{a} = \dfrac{\sin B}{b} = \dfrac{\sin C}{c}$ where A, B, and C are the angles in the triangle, and a, b, and c are the lengths of the sides opposite each of these angles.

124. What is the degree measure of the largest angle of a triangle that has sides of length 7, 8, and 9?

    (A) 75°
    (B) 73.398°
    (C) 16.602°
    (D) 15.945°
    (E) 1.281°

* Let's draw a picture

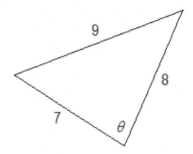

Note that the largest angle in a triangle is always opposite the longest side. So we are looking for θ in the figure above. We use the law of cosines.

$$9^2 = 7^2 + 8^2 - 2(7)(8)\cos\theta$$
$$81 = 113 - 112\cos\theta$$
$$-32 = -112\cos\theta$$
$$\cos\theta \approx 0.286$$
$$\theta \approx \cos^{-1} 0.286 \approx 73.398°$$

This is choice (B).

Note: The **Law of Cosines** says $c^2 = a^2 + b^2 - 2ab\cos C$ where a, b, and c are the lengths of the sides of the triangle, and the side of length c is opposite angle C.

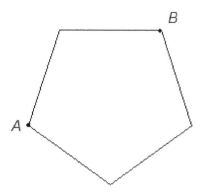

125. The figure above shows a regular pentagon with side length of 5. What is the length of $\overline{AB}$?

    (A) 6.01
    (B) 6.23
    (C) 7.56
    (D) 8.09
    (E) 8.91

* The total number of degrees in the interior of a pentagon is 540. So the degree measure of one angle in the pentagon is $\frac{540}{5} = 108°$. So we have the following picture.

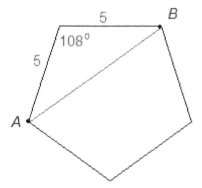

We now use the law of cosines to find AB.

$$AB^2 = 5^2 + 5^2 - 2(5)(5)\cos 108°$$

So $AB = \sqrt{25 + 25 - 50 \cos 108°} \approx 8.09$, choice (D).

115

Note: A **regular** polygon is a polygon with all sides equal in length, and all angles equal in measure.

The total number of degrees in the interior of an n-sided polygon is

$$(n-2) \cdot 180$$

For example, the number of degrees in the interior of a pentagon (5-sided polygon) is $(5-2) \cdot 180 = 3 \cdot 180 = 540$.

126. The vertex of $\angle P$ is the origin of the standard (x, y) coordinate plane. One ray of $\angle P$ is the positive x-axis. The other ray, $\overrightarrow{PQ}$, is positioned so that $\tan A < 0$ and $\sin A > 0$. In which quadrant, if it can be determined, is point Q ?

    (A) Quadrant I
    (B) Quadrant II
    (C) Quadrant III
    (D) Quadrant IV
    (E) Cannot be determined from the given information

* $\sin A > 0$ in Quadrants I and II and $\tan A < 0$ in Quadrants II and IV. So point Q must be in Quadrant II, choice (B).

Note: Many students find it helpful to remember the following diagram.

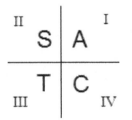

This diagram tells us which trig functions are positive in which quadrants. The **A** stands for "all" so that all trig functions are positive in the first quadrant. Similarly, **S** stands for "sine," **T** stands for "tangent," and **C** stands for "cosine."

So, for example, if an angle A in **standard position** (this just means that its initial side is the positive x-axis) has its terminal side in the second quadrant, then $\sin A > 0$, $\tan A < 0$ and $\cos A < 0$.

Exercise: Let A be an angle in standard position with terminal side in Quadrant I. For each of the six trig functions, determine if applying that function to A will give a positive or negative answer.

116

Repeat this exercise for Quadrants II, III and IV.

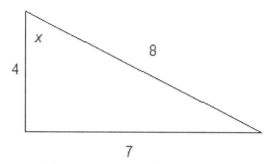

Note: Figure not drawn to scale.

127. In the figure above, what is the value of x in degrees?

(A) 47.5
(B) 52.1
(C) 56.4
(D) 61.0
(E) 75.9

* We use the law of cosines to get

$$7^2 = 4^2 + 8^2 - 2(4)(8)\cos x$$
$$49 = 16 + 64 - 64\cos x$$
$$-31 = -64\cos x$$
$$\cos x = \frac{-31}{-64} = \frac{31}{64}$$
$$x = \cos^{-1}\frac{31}{64} \approx 61$$

This is choice (D).

Notes: (1) The **Law of Cosines** says $c^2 = a^2 + b^2 - 2ab\cos C$ where a, b, and c are the lengths of the sides of the triangle, and the side of length c is opposite angle C.

(2) Observe that 7^2 is by itself on one side of the equation because the side of length 7 is opposite angle x.

(3) Don't be tricked into thinking this is a right triangle. Note that $8^2 = 64$ and $4^2 + 7^2 = 65$. So the Pythagorean Theorem is **not** satisfied.

128. For $0 < x < \frac{\pi}{2}$, the expression $\dfrac{\sin x}{\sqrt{1-\sin^2 x}} - \dfrac{\sqrt{1-\sin^2 x}}{\cos x}$ is equivalent to

    (A) $\tan x$
    (B) $\cot x$
    (C) $\tan x - 1$
    (D) $1 - \tan x$
    (E) $1 - \cot x$

* Since $1 - \sin^2 x = \cos^2 x$, we have

$$\frac{\sin x}{\sqrt{1-\sin^2 x}} - \frac{\sqrt{1-\sin^2 x}}{\cos x} = \frac{\sin x}{\sqrt{\cos^2 x}} - \frac{\sqrt{\cos^2 x}}{\cos x} = \frac{\sin x}{\cos x} - \frac{\cos x}{\cos x} = \tan x - 1$$

This is choice (C).

Note: (1) One of the most important trigonometric identities is the Pythagorean Identity which says

$$\cos^2 x + \sin^2 x = 1.$$

From this we also get the equations

$$\sin^2 x = 1 - \cos^2 x \quad \text{and} \quad \cos^2 x = 1 - \sin^2 x$$

by performing a simple subtraction.

(2) Since $0 < x < \frac{\pi}{2}$, $\cos x$ is positive. So $\sqrt{\cos^2 x} = \cos x$. If we didn't have a restriction on x, then we could only say $\sqrt{\cos^2 x} = |\cos x|$.

(3) We also needed the simple Quotient Identity $\frac{\sin x}{\cos x} = \tan x$.

(4) This problem could also be solved by picking numbers.

LEVEL 5: NUMBER THEORY

129. If a and b are positive integers, $\left(a^{\frac{1}{2}}b^{\frac{1}{3}}c^{\frac{1}{5}}\right)^{30} = 41{,}472$, and $abc = 1$, what is the value of ab?

    (A) 2
    (B) 3
    (C) 6
    (D) 8
    (E) 12

* $(a^{1/2}b^{1/3}c^{1/5})^{30} = a^{15}b^{10}c^6 = (abc)^6(ab)^4a^5 = (ab)^4a^5$. So we have that $(ab)^4a^5 = 41{,}472$. Since a and b are positive integers, ab must be a positive integer. So let's begin trying positive integer values for ab.

If $ab = 1$, then $a^5 = 41{,}472$. So $a = (41{,}472)^{1/5}$ which is not an integer. Let's try $ab = 2$ next. Then $a^5 = \frac{41{,}472}{2^4} = 2592$. So $a = 2592^{1/2}$ which is also not an integer. Setting ab equal to 3, 4, and 5 also do not work. But if we let $ab = 6$, then $a^5 = \frac{41{,}472}{6^4} = 32$. So $a = 2$, and thus, $b = 3$. So a and b are both integers. Therefore, $ab = 6$, choice (C).

Note: It turns out that c is not an integer $(c = \frac{1}{6})$.

130. If vector **u** has components $(-2,5)$, vector **v** has components $(3,1)$, and vector **w** has components $(0,-4)$, what is the magnitude of the vector $2\mathbf{u} - \mathbf{v} + 3\mathbf{w}$?

(A) 6.2
(B) 6.8
(C) 7.6
(D) 7.9
(E) 8.2

* $2\mathbf{u} = 2(-2,5) = (-4,10)$ and $3\mathbf{w} = 3(0,-4) = (0,-12)$. Therefore, we have $2\mathbf{u} - \mathbf{v} + 3\mathbf{w} = (-4,10) - (3,1) + (0,-12) = (-7,-3)$. The magnitude of $(-7,-3)$ is $\sqrt{(-7)^2 + (-3)^2} = \sqrt{49 + 9} = \sqrt{58} \approx 7.6$, choice (C).

131. The sum of the integers from 24 to 276, inclusive, is

(A) 37,950
(B) 28,462
(C) 18,975
(D) 12,325
(E) 8,125

* **Solution using the arithmetic series formula:** We multiply the number of terms we are adding by the average of the first and last term. The number of terms is $276 - 24 + 1 = 253$, and the average of the first and last term is $\frac{24+276}{2} = 150$. So the answer is $(253)(150) = 37{,}950$, choice (A).

Notes: (1) The sum of the terms of a sequence is called a **series**. A series is **arithmetic** if any two consecutive terms have the same difference.

(2) There is a simple formula for the sum of an arithmetic series:

$A_n = n \cdot m$ where n is the number of terms and m is the average (arithmetic mean) of the first and last term.

(3) The number of integers from a to b, inclusive, is $b - a + 1$. I call this the **fence-post formula**.

For example, let's count the number of integers from 5 to 12, inclusive. They are 5, 6, 7, 8, 9, 10, 11, 12, and we see that there are 8 of them. Now $12 - 5 = 7$ which is not the correct amount, but $12 - 5 + 1 = 8$ which is the correct amount.

If you ever happen to forget this little formula, test it out on a small list of numbers as I just did. But it's nice to have this one committed to memory so that it is there for you when you need it.

Solution using Gauss's technique: We formally write out this sum forward and backward, and then add.

$$24 + 25 + \ldots + 275 + 276$$
$$\underline{276 + 275 + \ldots + 25 + 24}$$
$$300 + 300 + \ldots + 300 + 300$$

By the fence-post formula we are adding 300 to itself $276 - 24 + 1 = 253$ times. This gives $300(253) = 75,900$. Since we added the sum twice we now divide by 2 to get \37,950, choice (A).

Note: This technique is used to derive the arithmetic sequence formula above.

Solution using a TI-84 calculator: Press the **2nd** button followed by the **List** button (same as **Stat** button).

Go to **Math** and select **5: sum(** or press **5**.

Press **2nd** followed by **List** again.

Go to **Ops** and select **5: seq(** or press **5**.

Enter **X, X, 24, 276))**.

The display should look like this:

sum(seq(X, X, 24, 276))

Press **Enter** and you should get the answer 37,950, choice (A).

Note: You do not need to type the closing parentheses. It is okay to enter

120

sum(seq(X, X, 24, 276 instead of **sum(seq(X, X, 24, 276))**.

132. If $a > 0$ and $b > 1$, then $\log_b \sqrt{a} =$

(A) $\log_{b^2} 2a$
(B) $\log_{b^2} a$
(C) $\log_{b^2} a^2$
(D) $\log_{2b} a^2$
(E) $\log_{2b} a$

* If $x = \log_b \sqrt{a}$, then $b^x = \sqrt{a}$. So $(b^2)^x = (b^x)^2 = a$. Therefore, $x = \log_{b^2} a$. So $\log_b \sqrt{a} = \log_{b^2} a$, choice (B).

Note: For more information on logarithms see problem 8.

LEVEL 5: ALGEBRA AND FUNCTIONS

133. If matrix M has dimensions $m \times n$, matrix N has dimensions $n \times p$, and matrix P has dimensions $p \times q$, which of the following statements is FALSE?

(A) The product MN exists.
(B) The product MNP exists and has dimensions $m \times q$.
(C) If $q = n$, then the product PN exists.
(D) The product PNM cannot exist.
(E) If the sum $M + N$ exists, then $m = n = p$.

* **Quick solution:** If $m = n = p = q$, then any of the given matrices can be multiplied in any order. In particular, PNM exists, and the answer is choice (D).

Notes: (1) If A is an $m \times n$ matrix, and B is a $p \times q$ matrix, then the product AB is defined if and only if $n = p$. In the given problem, the product MN and NP definitely exist, whereas the product MP only exists if $n = p$.

(2) Only matrices of the same size can be added. So if A is an $m \times n$ matrix, and B is a $p \times q$ matrix, then the sum $A + B$ is defined if and only if $m = p$ and $n = q$.

134. Which of the following transformations of the graph of $y = x^2$ would result in the graph of $y = -x^2 + 4x + k$ where k is a constant less than -4 ?

 (A) Shift right 2 units and up $-(k + 4)$ units.
 (B) Shift right 2 units and down $-(k + 4)$ units.
 (C) Reflect in y-axis, then shift left 2 units and up $-(k + 4)$ units.
 (D) Reflect in x-axis, then shift right 2 units and up $-(k + 4)$ units.
 (E) Reflect in x-axis, then shift right 2 units and down $-(k + 4)$ units.

* Solution by completing the square: We first factor out the minus sign from the first two terms on the right hand side.

$$y = -(x^2 - 4x) + k$$

We now take half of -4, which is -2, and square this number to get 4. We then add 4 inside the parentheses. Note that by distributing the minus sign, this means we are actually subtracting 4, so we add back 4 outside the parentheses as well.

$$y = -(x^2 - 4x + 4) + k + 4$$

The expression in parentheses is now the perfect square $(x - 2)^2$. So we have

$$y = -(x - 2)^2 + k + 4$$

Since we are given that $k < -4$, we have $k + 4 < 0$.

So the new graph is reflected in the x-axis, shifted 2 units right, and down $-(k + 4)$ units, choice **(E)**

Notes: (1) For a review of basic transformations see problem 101.

(2) The shift down is a bit tricky. Since $k + 4$ is a negative number we do not shift down $k + 4$ (this would technically be a shift up). We shift down $|k + 4|$ which is $-(k + 4)$.

(3) It may be helpful to see the transformation being applied one at a time:

Starting with $y = x^2$ we reflect in the x-axis by negating the function:

$$y = -x^2.$$

We next shift right 2 units by replacing x by $x - 2$:

$$y = -(x - 2)^2.$$

Finally, we shift down $-(k + 4)$ units by subtracting $-(k + 4)$:

$$y = -(x - 2)^2 - (-(k + 4)) = -(x - 2)^2 + k + 4$$

135. Let f be a linear function such that $f(5) = -2$ and $f(11) = 28$. What is the value of $\dfrac{f(9) - f(7)}{2}$?

    (A) 5
    (B) 4
    (C) 3
    (D) 2
    (E) 1

* The graph of f is a line with slope

$$\frac{f(11) - f(5)}{11 - 5} = \frac{28 - (-2)}{6} = \frac{30}{6} = 5.$$

But the slope of the line is also $\dfrac{f(9) - f(7)}{9 - 7} = \dfrac{f(9) - f(7)}{2}$. So the answer is 5, choice (A).

136. Suppose that z varies directly as x^2 and inversely as y^3. If $z = 9$ when $x = 3$ and $y = 2$, what is y when $z = 4.5$ and $x = 6$?

    (A) 2.5
    (B) 3.0
    (C) 3.5
    (D) 4.0
    (E) 4.5

* We are given that $z = \dfrac{kx^2}{y^3}$ for some constant k. Since $z = 9$ when $x = 3$ and $y = 2$, we have $9 = \dfrac{k(3)^2}{2^3} = \dfrac{9k}{8}$. So $k = 8$, and $z = \dfrac{8x^2}{y^3}$. We now substitute $z = 4.5$ and $x = 6$ to get $4.5 = \dfrac{8(6)^2}{y^3}$. So $y^3 = \dfrac{8(36)}{4.5} = 64$, and therefore $y = 4$, choice (D).

137. If $2x + 3y - 4z = 2$, $x - y + 5z = 6$ and $3x + 2y - z = 4$, what is the value of y ?

    (A) -0.4
    (B) 2
    (C) 3.6
    (D) 4.2
    (E) 5.1

* Solution using Gauss-Jordan reduction: Push the MATRIX button, scroll over to EDIT and then select [A] (or press 1). We will be inputting a 3 × 4 matrix, so press 3 ENTER 4 ENTER. Then enter the numbers 2, 3, −4 and 2 for the first row, 1, −1, 5 and 6 for the second row, and 3, 2, −1 and 4 for the third row.

Now push the QUIT button (2ND MODE) to get a blank screen. Press MATRIX again. This time scroll over to MATH and select rref((or press B). Then press MATRIX again and select [A] (or press 1) and press ENTER.

The display will show the following.

$$[\,[1\ 0\ 0\ -.4]$$
$$[0\ 1\ 0\ \ 3.6\,]$$
$$[0\ 0\ 1\ \ \ \ 2]\,]$$

The second line is interpreted as $y = 3.6$, choice (C).

138. The graphs of $y = bx^2$ and $y = k - bx^2$ intersect at points A and B. If the length of $\overline{AB}$ is equal to d, what is the value of $\frac{bd^2}{k}$?

    (A) 1
    (B) 2
    (C) 3
    (D) 4
    (E) 5

* Let's begin by drawing a picture.

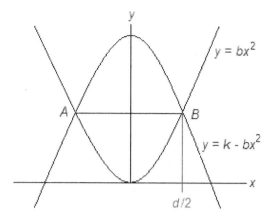

First note that the x-coordinate of point B is $\frac{d}{2}$. Since the two graphs intersect at B, we have $b(\frac{d}{2})^2 = k - b(\frac{d}{2})^2$. So $2b(\frac{d}{2})^2 = k$. Thus, $\frac{2bd^2}{2^2} = k$, so $bd^2=2k$, and therefore $\frac{bd^2}{k} = 2$, choice (B).

139. Let f and g be functions such that $f(x) = ax^2 + bx + c$ and $g(x) = ax + b$. If $g(1) = 2b - a + 25$ and $g(2) = 2a - 24$, then for what value of x does $f(x) = f(8)$, where $x \neq 8$?

   (A) 12
   (B) 16
   (C) 28
   (D) 32
   (E) 40

* $g(1) = a(1) + b = a + b$. So $a + b = 2b - a + 25$, and so $2a = b + 25$. $g(2) = a(2) + b = 2a + b$, and so $2a + b = 2a - 24$. Thus, $b = -24$. We also have $2a = b + 25 = -24 + 25 = 1$. Thus, $a = \frac{1}{2}$.

It follows that $f(x) = \frac{x^2}{2} - 24x + c$, and $f(8) = \frac{8^2}{2} - 24(8) + c = -160 + c$. If $f(x) = f(8)$, then $\frac{x^2}{2} - 24x + c = -160 + c$, and so $\frac{x^2}{2} - 24x + 160 = 0$. Let's multiply each side of this equation by 2 to eliminate the denominator. We get $x^2 - 48x + 320 = 0$. There are several ways to solve this equation.

Factoring: $(x - 8)(x - 40) = 0$. So $x = 40$, choice (E).

Completing the square: We take half of -48, which is -24, and square this number to get 576. We then add 576 to each side of the equation to get $x^2 - 48x + 576 + 320 = 576$. This is equivalent to $(x - 24)^2 = 256$. We now apply the square root property to get $x - 24 = \pm 16$. So $x = 24 \pm 16$. This yields the two solutions $24 - 16 = 8$, and $24 + 16 = 40$, choice (E).

The quadratic formula:

$$x = \frac{-b \pm \sqrt{b^2 - 4ac}}{2a} = \frac{48 \pm \sqrt{2304 - 1280}}{2} = \frac{48 \pm \sqrt{1024}}{2} = \frac{48 \pm 32}{2} = \mathbf{24 \pm 16.}$$

As in the previous solution we get $x = 8$ or $x = 40$, choice (E).

Graphically: In your graphing calculator press the Y= button, and enter the following.

$$Y1 = X^2 - 48X + 320$$

Now press ZOOM 6 to graph the parabola in a standard window. It needs to be zoomed out, so we will need to extend the viewing window. Press the WINDOW button, and change Xmax to 100, Ymin to −50, and Ymax to 50. Then press 2nd TRACE (which is CALC) 2 (or select ZERO). Then move the cursor just to the left of the second x-intercept and press ENTER. Now move the cursor just to the right of the second x-intercept and press ENTER again. Press ENTER once more, and you will see that the x-coordinate of the second x-intercept is 40, choice (E).

Remark: The choices made for Xmax, Ymin and Ymax were just to try to ensure that the second x-intercept would appear in the viewing window. Many other windows would work just as well.

140. If x and y are positive integers with $x^8 = \dfrac{z^3}{16}$ and $x^{12} = \dfrac{z^7}{y^4}$, what is the value of $\dfrac{xy}{z}$?

    (A) 5
    (B) 4
    (C) 3
    (D) 2
    (E) 1

* $x^4 = \dfrac{x^{12}}{x^8} = \dfrac{z^7}{y^4} \div \dfrac{z^3}{16} = \dfrac{z^7}{y^4} \cdot \dfrac{16}{z^3} = \dfrac{16z^4}{y^4}$. So $x = \dfrac{2z}{y}$, and so $\dfrac{xy}{z} = 2$, choice (D).

LEVEL 5: GEOMETRY

141. The circumference of the base of a right circular cone is 10π and the circumference of a parallel cross section is 8π. If the distance between the base and the cross section is 6, what is the height of the cone?

    (A) 12.5
    (B) 18
    (C) 22
    (D) 26
    (E) 30

* Let's start by drawing a picture.

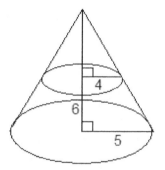

Since the circumference of the base of the cone is 10π, the radius is 5. Similarly, since the circumference of a parallel cross section is 8π, its radius is 4. We now have a pair of similar right triangles. If we let h be the height of the larger triangle, then the height of the smaller triangle is $h - 6$, and we get the ratio

$$\frac{h - 6}{h} = \frac{4}{5}$$

Cross multiplying, we get $5h - 30 = 4h$, and so $h = 30$, choice (E).

Note: The **circumference** of a circle with radius r is $C = 2\pi r$. So, for example, if the circumference is $C = 10\pi$, then $2\pi r = 10\pi$, and so we have $r = \frac{10\pi}{2\pi} = 5$.

127

142. If 432 distinct planes intersect in a line, and another line k intersects one of these planes in a single point, what is the least number of these 432 planes that k can intersect?

(A) 215
(B) 216
(C) 430
(D) 431
(E) 432

* Two parallel planes do not intersect. Therefore, none of the given planes are parallel. It follows that the line must either intersect all of these planes or the line will miss exactly one of these planes. So the line intersects 432 or 431 of these planes. The least number it can intersect is therefore 431, choice (D).

143. If the radius of the base of a right circular cylinder is increased by 10 percent, by what percent must the height be decreased so that the volume of the cylinder is decreased by 5 percent?

(A) 18.0%
(B) 21.5%
(C) 32.2%
(D) 39.0%
(E) 78.5%

* **Solution by picking numbers:** Let's start with a radius and height of 10 so that the volume is $V = \pi r^2 h = 1000\pi$. We now increase the radius by 10 percent, so that $r = 11$, and we decrease the volume by 5 percent, so that $V = 950\pi$. So we have

$$950\pi = \pi(11)^2 h$$
$$950 = 121h$$
$$h = \frac{950}{121} \approx 7.85$$

This is a decrease of $\frac{10-7.85}{10} \times 100 = 21.5$ percent, choice (B).

Note: Recall the formula for percent change:

$$Percent\ Change = \frac{Change}{Original} \times 100$$

128

144. Suppose that quadrilateral $PQRS$ has four congruent sides and satisfies $PQ = PR$. What is the value of $\frac{QS}{PR}$?

(A) $\frac{1}{2}$

(B) 1

(C) $\frac{\sqrt{3}}{2}$

(D) $\sqrt{2}$

(E) $\sqrt{3}$

* **Solution by picking a number:** Note that the quadrilateral is a rhombus. Let's draw a picture.

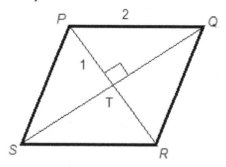

Now, let's choose a value for PQ, say $PQ = 2$. Since $PQ = PR$, $PR = 2$ as well. In a rhombus, the diagonals bisect each other, and are perpendicular to each other. It follows that $PT = 1$ and angle PTQ is a right angle. So triangle PTQ is a 30, 60, 90 triangle, and $QT = \sqrt{3}$. Thus, $QS = 2\sqrt{3}$, and it follows that $\frac{QS}{PR} = \frac{2\sqrt{3}}{2} = \sqrt{3}$, choice (E).

Direct solution: If we let $PT = x$, then $PQ = 2x$, and by a similar argument to the solution above we have $PR = 2x$ and $QS = 2x\sqrt{3}$. It follows that $\frac{QS}{PR} = \frac{2x\sqrt{3}}{2x} = \sqrt{3}$, choice (E).

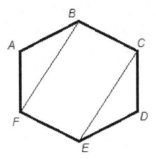

145. In the figure above, $ABCDEF$ is a regular hexagon and $CD = 6$. What is the perimeter of rectangle $BCEF$ to the nearest tenth?

  (A) 25.1
  (B) 28.3
  (C) 32.8
  (D) 35.6
  (E) 42.4

* Since the hexagon is regular, $BC = EF = CD = 6$. Now let's add a bit to the picture.

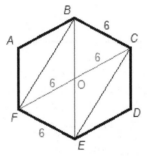

Again, note that the hexagon is regular. So each angle of triangle BOC is 60 degrees. Thus, triangle BOC is equilateral. So $OF = OC = BC = 6$. Since $EF = 6$ and $FC = 12$, triangle CEF is a 30, 60, 90 triangle. It follows that $CE = 6\sqrt{3}$. Since $BCEF$ is a rectangle, $BF = 6\sqrt{3}$ as well. So the perimeter of rectangle is $6 + 6 + 6\sqrt{3} + 6\sqrt{3} = 12 + 12\sqrt{3} \approx 32.78$. To the nearest tenth the answer is 32.8, choice (C).

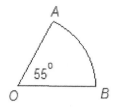

146. In the figure above, AB is the arc of a circle with center O. If the length of arc AB is 7π, what is the area of region OAB to the nearest integer?

(A) 252
(B) 251
(C) 250
(D) 249
(E) 248

* We first find the circumference of the circle using the ratio $\frac{55}{360} = \frac{7\pi}{C}$.

Cross multiplying gives $55C = 2520\pi$, so that $C = \frac{2520\pi}{55} = \frac{504\pi}{11}$. Since $C = 2\pi r$, we have $2\pi r = \frac{504\pi}{11}$, so $r = \frac{252}{11}$. The area of the circle is then $A = \pi r^2 = \frac{63,504\pi}{121}$. Now we find the area of the sector using the ratio $\frac{55}{360} \approx \frac{a}{524.8264463\pi}$. Cross multiplying gives us $360a \approx 28,865.45455\pi$. So $a \approx \frac{28,865.45455\pi}{360} \approx 252.$, choice (A).

147. An isosceles right triangle, T_1, has a hypotenuse of length $10\sqrt{2}$ units. The vertices of a second right triangle, T_2, are the midpoints of the sides of T_1. The vertices of a third right triangle, T_3, are the midpoints of the sides of T_2. This process continues indefinitely, with the vertices of T_{k+1} being the midpoints of the sides of T_k for each integer $k > 0$. What is the sum of the areas, in square units, of $T_1, T_2, ...$?

(A) $\frac{25}{3}$

(B) $\frac{50}{3}$

(C) $\frac{100}{3}$

(D) $\frac{200}{3}$

(E) 200

131

* Let's draw a picture of the first few triangles.

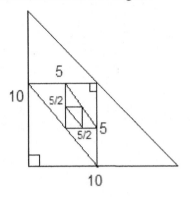

Note that an isosceles right triangle is the same as a 45, 45, 90 triangle. Since the hypotenuse of T_1 has length $10\sqrt{2}$, each leg has length 10, and therefore the area of T_1 is $\frac{1}{2}(10)(10) = 50$.

The legs of T_2 have lengths that are half the lengths of the legs of T_1. So each leg of T_2 has length 5, and the area of T_2 is $\frac{1}{2}(5)(5) = \frac{25}{2}$.

Let's do one more in case you don't see the pattern yet. The legs of T_3 have length $\frac{5}{2}$ so that the area of T_3 is $\frac{1}{2}(\frac{5}{2})(\frac{5}{2}) = \frac{25}{8}$.

So we want to compute the sum $50 + \frac{25}{2} + \frac{25}{8} + \cdots$

This is a geometric series with first term $g_1 = 50$ and common ratio $r = \frac{25}{2} \div 50 = \frac{1}{4}$. So the sum is $\frac{g_1}{1-r} = \frac{50}{1-\frac{1}{4}} = \frac{50}{\frac{3}{4}} = 50 \cdot \frac{4}{3} = \frac{200}{3}$, choice (D).

Note: It is okay to use a calculator for all of these computations.

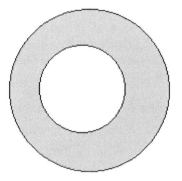

148. A circular disk is cut out of a larger circular disk, as shown in the figure above, so that the area of the piece that remains is the same as the area of the cutout. If the radius of the larger circle is R, what is the circumference of the cutout, in terms of R ?

   (A) R
   (B) $R\pi$
   (C) $R\sqrt{2}$
   (D) $R\pi\sqrt{2}$
   (E) $2R\pi\sqrt{2}$

* Let's let r be the radius of the cutout. Then the area of the small circle is πr^2 and the area of the piece that remains (shaded part) is $\pi R^2 - \pi r^2$. We are given that these two areas are equal so that $\pi R^2 - \pi r^2 = \pi r^2$. Adding πr^2 to each side of this equation gives $\pi R^2 = 2\pi r^2$. We now divide each side of this equation by 2π to get $\dfrac{R^2}{2} = r^2$. Taking the positive square root of each side yields $\dfrac{R}{\sqrt{2}} = r$. The circumference of the cutout is therefore $2\pi r = 2\pi \dfrac{R}{\sqrt{2}}$ This is equal to $R\pi\sqrt{2}$ (see Notes (4), (5) below), choice (D).

Notes: (1) The **circumference** of a circle with radius r is $C = 2\pi r$ and the **area** of a circle with radius r is $A = \pi r^2$.

(2) In this problem we are looking at two circles. The large circle is referred to as the "larger circular disk" in the problem and it has radius R. Therefore, its area is πR^2.

The small circle is referred to as both "a circular disk" and "the cutout" in the problem. In the solution we named its radius r. Therefore, its area is πr^2 and its circumference is $2\pi r$.

(3) The shaded region is referred to as "the piece that remains" in the problem and we can find its area by subtracting the area of the large circle minus the area of the small circle. This is a typical computation in **problems with shaded regions**. In this case the area of the shaded region is $\pi R^2 - \pi r^2$.

(4) Once we get the answer $2\pi\frac{R}{\sqrt{2}}$, we see that this is not an answer choice. We can simply ignore the R (since it's in every answer choice) and put $2\pi\frac{1}{\sqrt{2}}$ into our calculator. Then do the same with all the answer choices until we get the one that "matches up." This will be choice (D).

(5) If you really want to make the answer $2\pi\frac{R}{\sqrt{2}}$ "match up" with one of the answer choices by hand, you can **rationalize the denominator** by multiplying both the numerator and denominator by $\sqrt{2}$. The computation looks like this: $2\pi\frac{R}{\sqrt{2}} \cdot \frac{\sqrt{2}}{\sqrt{2}} = 2\pi\frac{R\sqrt{2}}{2} = \pi R\sqrt{2} = R\pi\sqrt{2}$.

LEVEL 5: PROBABILITY AND STATISTICS

149. Suppose that the average (arithmetic mean) of a, b, and c is h, the average of b, c, and d is j, and the average of d and e is k. What is the average of a and e?

    (A) $h - j + k$

    (B) $\dfrac{3h+3j-2k}{2}$

    (C) $\dfrac{3h-3j+2k}{2}$

    (D) $\dfrac{3h-3j+2k}{5}$

    (E) $\dfrac{3h-3j+2k}{8}$

* **Solution by changing averages to sums:** We have that $a + b + c = 3h$, $b + c + d = 3j$, and $d + e = 2k$. If we subtract the second equation from the first, and then add the third equation we get $a + e = 3h - 3j + 2k$. So the average of a and e is $\dfrac{a + e}{2} = \dfrac{3h - 3j + 2k}{2}$, choice (C).

Solution by picking numbers: Let's choose values for a, b, c, d, and e, say $a = 1$, $b = 2$, $c = 3$, $d = 4$, and $e = 6$. Then $h = 2$, $j = 3$, $k = 5$ and the average of a and e is **3.5**. The answer choices become

(A) 4
(B) 2.5
(C) 3.5
(D) 1.4
(E) .875

Since A, B, D, and E came out incorrect, the answer is choice (C).

150. How many ways are there to line up 3 men and 3 women if two
people of the same gender are not allowed to stand next to each
other?

(A) 6
(B) 24
(C) 36
(D) 72
(E) 144

Solution using only the counting principle: There are 6 choices for the
first person in the line. For the second person there are only 3 choices
(since the second person must be a different gender from the first). The
third person must be the same gender as the first person, and so there are
2 choices. Similarly, there are 2 choices for the fourth person, only 1 for
the fifth, and 1 for the sixth. By the counting principle we get
$(6)(3)(2)(2)(1)(1) = 72$ choices. This is answer choice (D).

* **Solution using permutations:** There are $_3P_3 = 6$ ways to line up 3
boys and $_3P_3 = 6$ ways to line up 3 girls. Once we've lined up the boys
and girls we see that there are 2 ways to interleave them: BGBGBG and
GBGBGB. By the counting principle the answer is $(6)(6)(2) = 72$, choice
(D).

Note: See problem 53 for more information on the counting principle and
permutations.

151. If 2 real numbers between 0 and 10 are randomly chosen, what
is the probability that the distance between them is at least 7?

(A) 0.09
(B) 0.13
(C) 0.15
(D) 0.21
(E) 0.30

* Let a and b be the two real numbers chosen between 0 and 10. Consider the following picture.

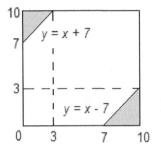

Note that we are trying to compute the probability that $|a - b| \geq 7$. This is equivalent to the two inequalities $a - b \leq -7$ and $a - b \geq 7$. Solving each of these inequalities for b gives $b \geq a + 7$ and $b \leq a - 7$. These inequalities correspond to the two shaded triangles in the figure above. The area of the shaded region is $2(\frac{1}{2})(3)(3) = 9$ and the area of the square is $10^2 = 100$. Therefore, the probability we are looking for is $\frac{9}{100} = 0.09$, choice (A).

152. A positive integer is called a palindrome if it reads the same forward as it does backward. For example, 1661 is a palindrome. If n is a positive integer, how many palindromes are there of length $2n + 1$?

    (A) n
    (B) 10^n
    (C) 10^{n+1}
    (D) $9 \cdot 10^n$
    (E) $9 \cdot 10^{2n}$

* **Solution by picking a number:** Let's let $n = 2$, so we are counting the number of palindromes of length $2(2) + 1 = 5$. We use the counting principle. There are 9 possibilities for the leftmost digit, 10 possibilities for the second digit from the left, and 10 possibilities for the middle digit. Since we are counting palindromes, the fourth and fifth digits from the left are determined by the second and first digits, respectively. So there are $9 \cdot 10 \cdot 10 = \mathbf{900}$ possibilities. We now substitute $n = 2$ into each answer choice.

(A) 2
(B) 100
(C) 1000
(D) 900
(E) 90,000

Since choices A, B, C, and E came out incorrect we can eliminate them and the answer is choice (D).

Notes: (1) See problem 53 for more information on the counting principle.

(2) The leftmost digit cannot be 0. That is why there are only 9 possibilities for this digit. All other digits that we choose can be 0, so there are 10 possibilities for each of the rest.

(3) A positive integer of the form $2n + 1$ is odd. Note that we get the integers 3, 5, 7... when we plug in $n = 1, 2, 3...$ and so on.

(4) An odd palindrome of length $2n + 1$ is determined by the first $n + 1$ digits. The first n are to the left of the centermost digit, and the $(n + 1)$st is in the center. The rightmost $n + 1$ must be the same as the leftmost $n + 1$. In particular, note that the rightmost digit cannot be 0 because it must be the same as the leftmost digit which cannot be 0.

LEVEL 5: TRIGONOMETRY

153. A ladder rests against the side of a wall and reaches a point that is 25 meters above the ground. The angle formed by the ladder and the ground is 58°. A point on the ladder is 3 meters from the wall. What is the vertical distance, in meters, from this point on the ladder to the ground?

    (A) $22 \tan 58°$
    (B) $22 \cos 58°$
    (C) $25 - 3 \sin 58°$
    (D) $25 - 3 \cos 58°$
    (E) $25 - 3 \tan 58°$

* Let's draw a picture.

137

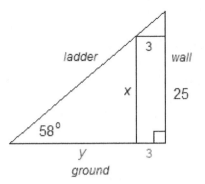

Note that we will be using two triangles in this picture: the triangle with sides of length x and y, and the triangle with sides lengths 25 and $y + 3$.

Also recall that for any angle A, $\tan A = \frac{\text{OPP}}{\text{ADJ}}$ (see the end of the solution to problem 25). Using the smaller triangle, we have $\tan 58° = \frac{x}{y}$ and using the larger triangle we have $\tan 58° = \frac{25}{y+3}$. The first equation gives $y \tan 58° = x$. and the second equation gives $(y + 3) \tan 58° = 25$. Distributing this last equation on the left gives $y \tan 58° + 3\tan 58° = 25$. Substituting from the first equation yields $x + 3 \tan 58° = 25$. We subtract $3\tan 58°$ from each side of this last equation to get $x = 25 - 3 \tan 58°$, choice (E).

154. If $\arcsin(\sin x) = \frac{\pi}{4}$ and $0 \le x \le 2\pi$, then x could equal

(A) 0

(B) $\frac{\pi}{6}$

(C) $\frac{\pi}{3}$

(D) $\frac{3\pi}{4}$

(E) $\frac{5\pi}{4}$

* x could certainly equal $\frac{\pi}{4}$ (see problem 90), but $\frac{\pi}{4}$ is not an answer choice. So we need to find $x \ne \frac{\pi}{4}$ so that $\sin x = \sin \frac{\pi}{4}$.

Since $\sin x > 0$ in quadrant II, we find the corresponding second quadrant angle. This is $\pi - \frac{\pi}{4} = \frac{4\pi - \pi}{4} = \frac{3\pi}{4}$, choice (D).

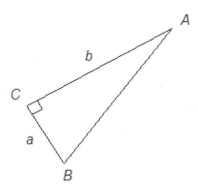

155. In the right triangle above, $b > a > 0$. One of the angle measures in the triangle is $\cos^{-1}\frac{b}{\sqrt{a^2+b^2}}$. What is $\csc[\cos^{-1}\left(\frac{b}{\sqrt{a^2+b^2}}\right)]$?

(A) $\dfrac{b}{a}$

(B) $\dfrac{a}{b}$

(C) $\dfrac{b}{\sqrt{a^2+b^2}}$

(D) $\dfrac{a}{\sqrt{a^2+b^2}}$

(E) $\dfrac{\sqrt{a^2+b^2}}{a}$

* First note that by the Pythagorean Theorem, $AB = \sqrt{a^2 + b^2}$. Since $\cos A = \frac{\text{ADJ}}{\text{HYP}} = \frac{b}{\sqrt{a^2+b^2}}$, it follows that $\cos^{-1}\frac{b}{\sqrt{a^2+b^2}} = A$. So we have $\csc[\cos^{-1}\left(\frac{b}{\sqrt{a^2+b^2}}\right)] = \csc A = \frac{\text{HYP}}{OPP} = \frac{\sqrt{a^2+b^2}}{a}$, choice (E).

Notes: (1) $\cos^{-1} x = y$ is essentially the same as $\cos y = x$ (more specifically, this is true for $0 \leq y \leq \pi$).

To compute $\cos y$ we input an angle and get out a number. To compute $\cos^{-1} x$ we input a number and get out an angle (in radians).

139

(2) We can get the answer to this problem in just a few seconds without any writing. Here is how to think about it. For the expression $\csc[\cos^{-1}\left(\frac{b}{\sqrt{a^2+b^2}}\right)]$, we are simply computing the cosecant of an angle. We just need to figure out if we want angle A or angle B. We choose the correct angle by looking at the cosine of each angle. We want the cosine of the angle to be $\frac{b}{\sqrt{a^2+b^2}}$. In other words, we just want the adjacent side to the angle to be b. Well this is angle A. So we just need to compute $\csc A$.

To summarize, since the side adjacent to A has length b, we simply compute $\csc A = \frac{\sqrt{a^2+b^2}}{a}$.

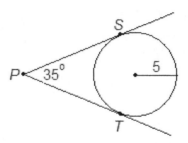

156. In the figure above, two lines are tangent to a circle of radius 5 at points S and T. What is the length of segment $\overline{ST}$ (not shown)?

   (A) 10
   (B) 9.91
   (C) 9.54
   (D) 9.02
   (E) 8.43

* Let's let x be the degree measure of major arc ST. Then the length of minor arc ST is $360° - x$, and we have

$$35° = \frac{x-(360°-x)}{2} = \frac{x-360°+x}{2} = \frac{2x-360°}{2}$$
$$70° = 2x - 360°$$
$$430° = 2x$$
$$215° = x$$

So the degree measure of minor arc ST is $360 - 215 = 145°$.

Let's add some information to the picture.

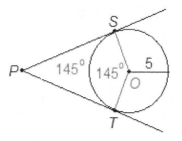

Note that central angle *SOT* has the same degree measure as the arc it intercepts.

Now let's draw in segment $\overline{ST}$.

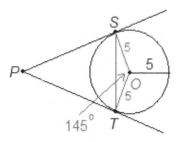

Note that $OS = OT = 5$, because these segments are radii of the circle. We can now use the law of cosines to find *ST*.

$$ST^2 = 5^2 + 5^2 - 2(5)(5)\cos 145°$$

So $ST = \sqrt{5^2 + 5^2 - 2(5)(5)\cos 145°} \approx 9.54$, choice (C).

Note: The **Law of Cosines** says $c^2 = a^2 + b^2 - 2ab\cos C$ where a, b, and c are the lengths of the sides of the triangle, and the side of length c is opposite angle C.

141

CHALLENGE PROBLEMS

157. Let $k = n^4 - 6n^2 + 1$ where n is a positive integer such that $n > 2$. Which of the following statements **must** be true:

I. $k = (n^2 - 2n - 1)(n^2 + 2n - 1)$
II. k is composite
III. k is odd.

   (A) I only
   (B) II only
   (C) III only
   (D) I and II only
   (E) I, II and III

$$n^4 - 6n^2 + 1 = (n^2 - 1)^2 - (2n)^2 = (n^2 - 1 - 2n)(n^2 - 1 + 2n)$$
$$= (n^2 - 2n - 1)(n^2 + 2n - 1).$$

So I must be true and we can eliminate choice B and C.

Note: We can also multiply $(n^2 - 2n - 1)(n^2 + 2n - 1)$ to get $n^4 - 6n^2 + 1$.

The expression $(n^2 - 2n - 1)(n^2 + 2n - 1)$ will be composite as long as each factor is not equal to 1 or -1. So we have to solve four equations.

$n^2 - 2n - 1 = 1$: Then $n^2 - 2n - 2 = 0$. This equation has discriminant $(-2)^2 - 4(1)(-2) = 12$. Since 12 is not a perfect square, this equation has no integer solutions. So there is no integer n with $n^2 - 2n - 1 = 1$.

$n^2 + 2n - 1 = 1$: Then $n^2 + 2n - 2 = 0$. This equation has discriminant $2^2 - 4(1)(-2) = 12$. Since 12 is not a perfect square, this equation has no integer solutions. So there is no integer n with $n^2 + 2n - 1 = 1$.

$n^2 - 2n - 1 = -1$: Then $n^2 - 2n = 0$. So $n(n - 2) = 0$, which has solutions $n = 0$ and $n = 2$. But we are assuming that $n > 2$.

$n^2 + 2n - 1 = -1$: Then $n^2 + 2n = 0$. So $n(n + 2) = 0$, which has solutions $n = 0$ and $n = -2$. But we are assuming that $n > 2$.

In summary, if n is an integer greater than 2, then $n^4 - 6n^2 + 1$ factors as

$$(n^2 - 2n - 1)(n^2 + 2n - 1)$$

And neither factor is equal to 1 or -1. Therefore $n^4 - 6n^2 + 1$ is composite.

So II must be true and we can eliminate choice (A).

Finally, if n is odd, then n^4 is odd. Since $6n^2$ is always even and 1 is odd, $n^4 - 6n^2 + 1$ is even (odd – even + odd = even).

So III does not have to be true, and the answer is choice (D).

Note: A single counterexample will suffice here. For example, if $n = 3$, then $k = n^4 - 6n^2 + 1 = 3^4 - 6(3)^2 + 1 = 28$ which is even.

158. Dr. Steve recently attended an event with his girlfriend. At this event there were two other couples. Some handshakes took place. No one shook his/her own hand, no one shook hands with his/her girlfriend/boyfriend, and no one shook hands with the same person twice. Later on Dr. Steve asked everyone at the event, including his girlfriend, how many hands he or she had shaken. Each person gave a different answer. How many hands did Dr. Steve's girlfriend shake?

   (A) 0
   (B) 1
   (C) 2
   (D) 3
   (E) 4

Label the people at the event as A, B, C, D, E and F. The answers to Dr. Steve's question must have been 0, 1, 2, 3 and 4.

So one person, let's say A, has shaken hands with 4 others, let's say B, C, D, and E. So we see that F has shaken hands with no one, and A and F are a couple.

Now, let's say B has shaken hands with 3 others. Well we already know A is one of them. So assume they are A, C and D. So E must have shaken hands with just one person, and B and E are a couple.

It follows that C and D are a couple and each shook hands with 2 others. Since these numbers are the same, one must be Dr. Steve. Thus the other is his girlfriend. So the answer is 2, choice (C).

159. How many arrangements of the word EFFLORESCENCE have consecutive C's and F's but no consecutive E's?

   (A) 70
   (B) 5040
   (C) 282,240
   (D) 352, 800
   (E) 924,000

* First place the E's. We need to place seven other "letters":

$$CC, FF, L, O, R, S, \text{ and } N.$$

To make things simpler let's imagine these are 7 different scrabble tiles. For now, turn all of them face down. Let's call them "non-E" tiles.

Place a non-E tile face down between the first and the second E, one non-E tile face down between the second and the third E and finally another non-E tile face down between the third and the fourth E. Now the E's are separated.

Place the remaining 4 non-E tiles wherever you want in the 5 regions determined by the E tiles. There are $_8C_4$ ways to do this. At this point you have a 13-letter word consisting of E tiles and non-E tiles.

Finally, turn the non-E tiles face up. Since they are all different there are 7! possible arrangements.

So the final answer is $1 \cdot 1 \cdot {_8C_4} \cdot 7! = 352,800$, choice (D).

** Thanks to Dan Ismailescu for providing this solution!

160. A cube is inscribed in a cone of radius 1 and height 2 so that one face of the cube is contained in the base of the cone. What is the length of a side of the cube?

   (A) $2\sqrt{2} - 2$
   (B) $2\sqrt{2} + 2$
   (C) $2\sqrt{3} - 2$
   (D) $2\sqrt{3} + 2$
   (E) $2\sqrt{3} - 3$

* Let x be the length of a side of the cube. Slice the cone from the vertex to the base so that it cuts through the diagonal of the square base of the cube. We get the following picture.

144

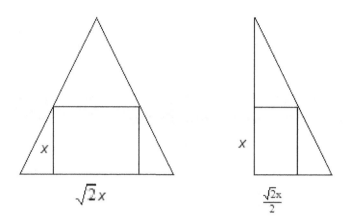

We can now set up the following ratio:

$$\frac{1}{2} = \frac{1 - \frac{\sqrt{2}x}{2}}{x}$$

Cross multiplying gives $x = 2 - \sqrt{2}\,x,$ or equivalently $x + \sqrt{2}\,x = 2.$ So

$$x\left(1 + \sqrt{2}\right) = 2 \qquad \text{and} \qquad x = \frac{2}{1+\sqrt{2}}$$

By rationalizing the denominator, this can be simplified to

$$x = 2\sqrt{2} - 2$$

145

SUPPLEMENTAL PROBLEMS
QUESTIONS

LEVEL 1: NUMBER THEORY

1. How many digits does the integer 5^{62} have?

   (A) 42
   (B) 43
   (C) 44
   (D) 45
   (E) 46

2. $\dfrac{n!(n+2)!}{(n+1)!(n-1)!} =$

   (A) n^2
   (B) $n^2 + 2n$
   (C) $n^2 + 2n + 1$
   (D) $n(n+1)$
   (E) $n(n+1)(n+2)$

3. In a geometric sequence, the third term is 4 and the fifth term is 9. What is the seventh term in the sequence?

   (A) 243

   (B) 81

   (C) 27

   (D) $\dfrac{27}{2}$

   (E) $\dfrac{81}{4}$

4. If a and b are even integers, then which of the following could be an odd integer?

   (A) $a + b$

   (B) $ab + b$

   (C) $a(b + 1)$

   (D) $(a + 1)(b - 1) + 1$

   (E) $\dfrac{a}{b}$

146

LEVEL 1: ALGEBRA AND FUNCTIONS

5.   What is the value of c^2 if $c = \sqrt{26^2 - 24^2}$?

   (A) $\sqrt{10}$
   (B) 10
   (C) 10^2
   (D) 100^2
   (E) 1000^2

6.   If $(x - 2)g(x) = x^3 - 5x^2 + 10x - 8$ where $g(x)$ is a polynomial in x, then $g(x) =$

   (A) $x + 4$
   (B) $x^2 + 4$
   (C) $x^2 + 4x$
   (D) $x^2 - 3x + 4$
   (E) $x^2 + 3x + 4$

7.   If $rs = 4, st = 7, rt = 63$, and $r > 0$, then $rst =$

   (A) 35
   (B) 40
   (C) 42
   (D) 60
   (E) 120

8. $\dfrac{5x(yz+z)-5xz}{-xyz} =$

   (A) -5
   (B) -4
   (C) -3
   (D) -2
   (E) -1

9.   If $k(x) = \dfrac{x^2-4}{x-2}$ and $h(x) = \dfrac{3\ln x^2}{8}$, then $h\big(k(e - 2)\big) =$

   (A) $.12$
   (B) $.5$
   (C) $.51$
   (D) $.75$
   (E) 1.25

147

10. How many roots does the function $f(x) = x^3 + x^2 - 2x$ have?

   (A) One
   (B) Two
   (C) Three
   (D) Four
   (E) More than four

11. For all real numbers a and b, $|b - a| - |a - b| =$

   (A) $2(a - b)$
   (B) $2b - 2a$
   (C) 0
   (D) $2b + 2a$
   (E) $2a + b$

12. If x varies inversely as y, and $x = 2$ when $y = 6$, then what is the value of y when $x = k$?

   (A) $12k^2$

   (B) $6k^2$

   (C) $12k$

   (D) $\frac{12}{k}$

   (E) $\frac{4}{k}$

LEVEL 1: GEOMETRY

13. What is the length of an edge of a cube whose volume and surface area are equal?

   (A) 2
   (B) 4
   (C) 6
   (D) 8
   (E) 10

14. What is the slope of the line passing through the points $(-2, -6)$ and $(-4,5)$?

    (A) 2

    (B) $\frac{1}{2}$

    (C) $-\frac{2}{11}$

    (D) $-\frac{11}{6}$

    (E) $-\frac{11}{2}$

15. The midpoint of PQ is $(3,1)$. If point P has coordinates $(5,-2)$, then what is the x-coordinate of point Q ?

    (A) -1

    (B) $-\frac{1}{2}$

    (C) 0

    (D) $\frac{1}{2}$

    (E) 1

16. If the base radius of cone S is one-half as long as the base radius of cone T and the heights of the two cones are equal, then the volume of cone S is what fraction of the volume of cone T ?

    (A) $\frac{1}{2}$

    (B) $\frac{1}{3}$

    (C) $\frac{1}{4}$

    (D) $\frac{1}{5}$

    (E) $\frac{1}{8}$

17. In the rectangular coordinate system, the point $P(a, b)$ is moved to the new point $Q(5a, 5b)$. What is the distance between points P and Q?

    (A) a

    (B) b

    (C) $\sqrt{a^2 + b^2}$

    (D) $2\sqrt{a^2 + b^2}$

    (E) $4\sqrt{a^2 + b^2}$

18. Which of the following is NOT a vertex of the ellipse whose equation is $\dfrac{(x-3)^2}{25} + \dfrac{(y+2)^2}{49} = 1$?

    (A) $(-2, -2)$
    (B) $(-2, 8)$
    (C) $(3, 5)$
    (D) $(3, -9)$
    (E) $(8, -2)$

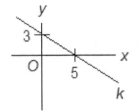

19. An equation of line k in the figure above is

    (A) $x = 5$

    (B) $y = 3$

    (C) $y = \dfrac{3}{5}x + 3$

    (D) $y = -\dfrac{3}{5}x + 3$

    (E) $y = \dfrac{5}{3x} + 3$

20. Lines k and n are distinct parallel lines. If line n passes through the points $(0,0)$ and $(3,2)$, then line k can pass through which of the following points?

    (A) $(-3,-2)$
    (B) $(-1,-3)$
    (C) $(6,4)$
    (D) $(9,6)$
    (E) $(15,10)$

LEVEL 1: PROBABILITY AND STATISTICS

21. The average (arithmetic mean) of z, 2, 16, and 21 is z. What is the value of z?

    (A) 12
    (B) 13
    (C) 14
    (D) 15
    (E) 16

22. In Bakerfield, 60 of the residents who own at least one cat also play the piano. If 200 residents of Bakerfield do not own a cat, and Bakerfield has 400 residents, how many residents own at least one cat but do not play the piano?

    (A) 100
    (B) 120
    (C) 140
    (D) 160
    (E) 180

23. If two six-sided dice are rolled, what is the probability that the sum of the two numbers will be 9?

    (A) $\frac{1}{9}$

    (B) $\frac{1}{8}$

    (C) $\frac{1}{6}$

    (D) $\frac{1}{4}$

    (E) $\frac{1}{3}$

24. From a group of 7 people, in how many ways can 4 be chosen?

    (A) 4
    (B) 7
    (C) 28
    (D) 35
    (E) 210

LEVEL 1: TRIGONOMETRY

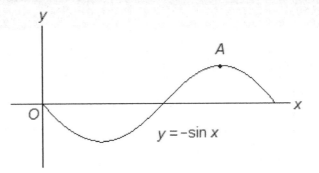

25. The figure above shows one cycle of the graph of the function $y = -\sin x$ for $0 \leq x \leq 2\pi$. If the maximum value of the function occurs at point A, then the coordinates of A are

    (A) $(\frac{\pi}{3}, \pi)$

    (B) $(\frac{\pi}{3}, 1)$

    (C) $(\frac{\pi}{3}, 0)$

    (D) $(\frac{\pi}{2}, \pi)$

    (E) $(\frac{3\pi}{2}, 1)$

26. If $\sin x = .03325$, then $\csc x =$

    (A) 11.7600
    (B) 14.2135
    (C) 18.0002
    (D) 22.3576
    (E) 30.0752

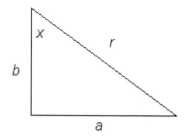

27. In the figure above, $r \sin x =$

    (A) a
    (B) b
    (C) r
    (D) $a + b$
    (E) ab

28. If $0 \le x \le \frac{\pi}{2}$ and $\tan x = \frac{1}{4}\tan\frac{5\pi}{16}$, then $x =$

    (A) 0.127
    (B) 0.358
    (C) 0.449
    (D) 0.611
    (E) 0.682

29. Whenever $\frac{\tan x}{\cos x}$ is defined, it is equivalent to:

    (A) $\cos x$
    (B) $\sin x$
    (C) $\dfrac{1}{\cos x}$
    (D) $\dfrac{1}{\sin x}$
    (E) $\dfrac{\sin x}{\cos^2 x}$

153

30. A dog, a cat, and a mouse are all sitting in a room. Their relative positions to each other are described in the figure below. Which of the following expressions gives the distance, in feet, from the cat to the dog?

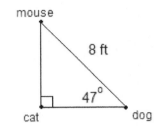

(A) 8 sin 47°

(B) 8 cos 47°

(C) 8 tan 47°

(D) $\dfrac{8}{\sin 47°}$

(E) $\dfrac{8}{\cos 47°}$

31. If $0 < x < \dfrac{\pi}{2}$ and $\tan x = 1.525$, what is the value of $\sec\left(\dfrac{x}{3}\right)$?

(A) 0.548
(B) 0.990
(C) 1.057
(D) 1.932
(E) 2.322

32. For any acute angle with measure A, $\csc(90° - A) =$

(A) $\sin A$
(B) $\cos A$
(C) $\tan A$
(D) $\csc A$
(E) $\sec A$

LEVEL 2: NUMBER THEORY

33. A sequence is recursively defined by $k_1 = 1$, $k_2 = 0$, and $k_n = k_{n-1}^2 + k_{n-2}$, for $n > 2$. What is the value of k_7 ?

    (A) 0
    (B) 1
    (C) 2
    (D) 5
    (E) 27

34. $\sum_{n=1}^{20} 2k + 4 =$

    (A) 50
    (B) 250
    (C) 400
    (D) 500
    (E) 1000

35. What is the sum of the infinite geometric series?

$$\frac{1}{9} + \frac{1}{27} + \frac{1}{81} + \frac{1}{243} + \cdots ?$$

    (A) $\frac{1}{81}$

    (B) $\frac{1}{27}$

    (C) $\frac{1}{15}$

    (D) $\frac{1}{12}$

    (E) $\frac{1}{6}$

36. If $e^k = 7$, then $k =$

    (A) 1.24
    (B) 1.33
    (C) 1.53
    (D) 1.88
    (E) 1.95

LEVEL 2: ALGEBRA AND FUNCTIONS

37. If $g(x) = 2^x$ and $f(x) = 5\log_2 x - 10$, then $g(f(8)) =$

    (A) 0
    (B) 1
    (C) 2
    (D) 16
    (E) 32

38. If a and b are in the domain of a function g and $g(a) = g(b)$, which of the following must be true?

    (A) $a = b$
    (B) g fails the vertical line test.
    (C) there is a horizontal line that intersects the graph of g at least twice.
    (D) the graph of g is a horizontal line.
    (E) The point (a, b) is on the graph of g.

39. If $f(x) = \sqrt{3 - x}$ and $g(x) = \frac{1}{x^2 - 1}$, what is the domain of fg ?

    (A) all real numbers x

    (B) all x such that $x \geq 3$

    (C) all x such that $x \neq 1$ and $x \leq 3$

    (D) all x such that $x \neq \pm 1$ and $x \leq 3$

    (E) all x such that $1 < x \leq 3$

40. If $x = \frac{2}{5}$ is a solution to the equation $3(x - 5)(10x - c) = 0$, what is the value of c ?

    (A) 4
    (B) 3
    (C) 2
    (D) 1
    (E) 0

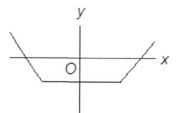

41. The graph of $y = h(x)$ is shown above. Which of the following could be the graph of $y = h(|x|)$?

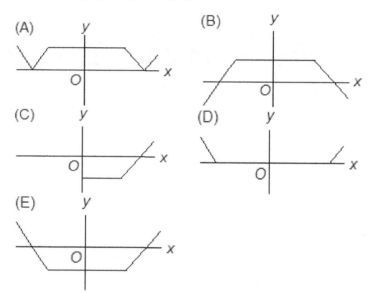

(A)

(B)

(C)

(D)

(E)

42. If $\ln x = 2.37$ then $\ln 5x^2 =$

    (A) 4.09
    (B) 5.22
    (C) 6.01
    (D) 6.35
    (E) 8.22

43. What value does $\dfrac{x^2-3x-10}{5x+10}$ approach as x approaches -2?

    (A) $-\dfrac{7}{5}$
    (B) -1
    (C) $-\dfrac{5}{7}$
    (D) $\dfrac{1}{5}$
    (E) 5

44. If $k(x) = \left(\sqrt{x} + 3\right)^3$, for all $x > 0$, then which of the following functions is equal to $f^{-1}(x)$ when restricted to $x > 27$?

    (A) $\sqrt[3]{x}$
    (B) $\sqrt[3]{x} - 3$
    (C) $\left(\sqrt[3]{x} - 3\right)^2$
    (D) $(x - 3)^2$
    (E) $(x - 3)^3$

LEVEL 2: GEOMETRY

45. The greatest possible distance between two vertices of a rectangular solid is 15. Which of the following could be the dimensions of the solid?

    (A) 3, 7, 11
    (B) 5, 6, 7
    (C) 5, 10, 10
    (D) 7, 7, 11
    (E) 9, 11, 13

46. A sphere has a radius of 6, and its center at the origin. Which of the following points is inside the sphere?

    (A) 3, 4, 5
    (B) 1, 3, 5
    (C) 2, 4, 4
    (D) 2, 2, 6
    (E) 1, 1, 7

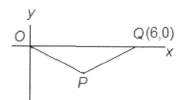

47. In the above triangle, if $OP = QP$ and $m\angle OPQ = 120°$, what is the slope of segment PQ?

(A) $\dfrac{1}{\sqrt{3}}$

(B) $\dfrac{1}{\sqrt{2}}$

(C) $\sqrt{2}$

(D) $\sqrt{3}$

(E) $3\sqrt{3}$

48. Which of the following is an equation whose graph is the set of points equidistant from the points $(2,-1)$ and $(2,5)$?

(A) $y = 2$
(B) $x = 2$
(C) $y = 3$
(D) $x = 3$
(E) $y = x + 2$

49. Which of the following is an equation of a line parallel to $3x + 2y = 5$?

(A) $y = -\dfrac{5}{2}x + \dfrac{5}{2}$

(B) $y = -\dfrac{3}{2}x + 1$

(C) $y = \dfrac{3}{2}x + 1$

(D) $y = \dfrac{2}{3}x + 1$

(E) $y = -\dfrac{2}{3}x + 1$

159

50. A cylinder is inscribed in a cube with an edge of length 4. What is the volume of the space enclosed by the cube, but NOT by the cylinder?

  (A) 11.5
  (B) 13.7
  (C) 14.0
  (D) 14.9
  (E) 15.3

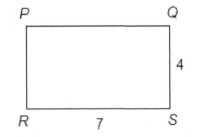

51. What is the volume of the solid generated by rotating rectangle *PQSR* around *QS* ?

  (A) 28π
  (B) 49π
  (C) 112π
  (D) 152π
  (E) 196π

52. What is the distance in space between the points with coordinates $(-6,4,5)$ and $(1,-1,-1)$?

  (A) 8.7
  (B) 10.5
  (C) 11.1
  (D) 11.7
  (E) 12.3

160

LEVEL 2: PROBABILITY AND STATISTICS

53. In a small town, 30 families have cats, 50 families have dogs, and 25 families have neither cats nor dogs. If there are 90 families living in the town, how many families have both cats and dogs?

    (A) 10
    (B) 15
    (C) 20
    (D) 25
    (E) 30

54. If two six-sided dice are rolled, what is the probability that the sum of the two numbers shown will be even?

    (A) $\frac{1}{2}$

    (B) $\frac{1}{3}$

    (C) $\frac{1}{4}$

    (D) $\frac{1}{6}$

    (E) $\frac{1}{9}$

55. In how many different ways can a line of 7 people be formed?

    (A) 7
    (B) 42
    (C) 49
    (D) 5040
    (E) 823,543

TEST GRADES OF STUDENTS IN MATH CLASS

Test Grade	75	82	87	93	100
Number of students with that grade	5	7	10	3	1

56. The test grades of the 26 students in a math class are shown in the chart above. What is the median test grade for the class?

   (A) 75
   (B) 82
   (C) 87
   (D) 90
   (E) 93

LEVEL 2: TRIGONOMETRY

57. To the nearest tenth of a degree, what is the measure of the smallest angle in a right triangle with sides 5, 12, and 13 ?

   (A) 22.6°
   (B) 32.1°
   (C) 41.7°
   (D) 52.0°
   (E) 55.8°

58. What is the range of the following function?

$$T(x) = -4\sin(2x + \pi) + 3$$

   (A) $-4 \leq x \leq 4$
   (B) $-4 \leq x \leq 7$
   (C) $-1 \leq x \leq 4$
   (D) $-1 \leq x \leq 7$
   (E) $-7 \leq x \leq 1$

59. $\sin x \tan x + \cos x =$

   (A) $\sin x$
   (B) $\cos x$
   (C) $\tan x$
   (D) $\cot x$
   (E) $\sec x$

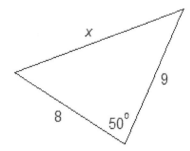

60. In the triangle shown above, $x =$

(A) 6.85
(B) 6.93
(C) 7.00
(D) 7.13
(E) 7.24

61. If $0 \leq x \leq 2\pi$, $\cot x > 0$ and $\sec x \cot x < 0$, then which of the following is a possible value for x ?

(A) $\frac{\pi}{6}$

(B) $\frac{\pi}{2}$

(C) $\frac{5\pi}{6}$

(D) $\frac{7\pi}{6}$

(E) $\frac{11\pi}{6}$

62. If $0 \leq x \leq \frac{\pi}{2}$ and $\csc x = 5 \sec x$, what is the value of $\tan x$?

(A) 0.2
(B) 1.0
(C) 3.0
(D) 4.2
(E) 5.0

163

63. $\dfrac{\sin x}{\cos x \tan x} =$

    (A) $\cot x$
    (B) $\csc x$
    (C) $\sec x$
    (D) $\cos x$
    (E) None of these

64. $(1 - \cos x)(1 + \cos x) =$

    (A) $\sin x$
    (B) $\cos x$
    (C) $\sin^2 x$
    (D) $\cos^2 x$
    (E) $\sec x \tan x$

LEVEL 3: NUMBER THEORY

65. A Fibonacci-type sequence can be defined recursively as $a_n = a_{n-1} + a_{n-2}$ for $n > 2$, and where a_1 and a_2 are given real numbers. What is the 8th term of the Fibonacci-type sequence where $a_1 = 2$ and $a_2 = 3$?

    (A) 21
    (B) 34
    (C) 55
    (D) 90
    (E) 146

If Stanley gets a 90 on his last test, then he will get an A.

66. Which of the following CANNOT be inferred from the statement above?

    (A) If Stanley gets an A, then he received a 90 on his last test.
    (B) If Stanley did not get an A, then he did not receive a 90 on his last test.
    (C) A necessary condition for Stanley to get a 90 on his last test is that he gets an A.
    (D) In order for Stanley to get an A, it is sufficient that he gets a 90 on his last test.
    (E) Stanley gets a 90 on his last test implies that he will get an A.

67. If $\log_4 x = k$, then $\log_2 x =$

    (A) $\dfrac{k}{2}$

    (B) $2k$

    (C) $4k$

    (D) k^2

    (E) 2^k

68. If $i^2 = -1$, then what is the value of i^{73} ?

    (A) 0
    (B) 1
    (C) -1
    (D) i
    (E) $-i$

LEVEL 3: ALGEBRA AND FUNCTIONS

69. The graph of the rational function r where $r(x) = \dfrac{x^2-1}{x^2-4}$ has asymptotes $x = a$, $x = b$, and $y = c$. What is the value of $a + b + c$?

    (A) $-\dfrac{1}{4}$

    (B) $\dfrac{1}{4}$

    (C) 1

    (D) 3

    (E) 5

70. What is the range of the function defined by $\dfrac{1}{x^2} - 2$?

    (A) All real numbers
    (B) All real numbers except 0
    (C) All real numbers except -2
    (D) All real numbers greater than 0
    (E) All real numbers greater than -2

71. If x varies inversely as y^2, and x is 3 when y is 5, then what is x when y is 3?

    (A) 3
    (B) 5
    (C) 8.3
    (D) 16.6
    (E) 25

72. $\dfrac{x^4+x^3+x^2}{x^7+x^6+x^5} =$

    (A) x^3

    (B) x

    (C) x^{-3}

    (D) $3x$

    (E) 3

73. Which of the following lines is an asymptote of the graph of $g(x) = 5\ln(x+2)$?

    (A) $y = -2$
    (B) $y = 0$
    (C) $x = -2$
    (D) $x = 0$
    (E) $x = 2$

74. If $ab^2c = 6$ and $a^2bc^3 = 27$, what is the value of $\dfrac{ac^2}{b}$?

    (A) 0.2
    (B) 3.0
    (C) 4.5
    (D) 5.4
    (E) 6.0

75. If matrix A has dimensions 5×7 and matrix B has dimensions 7×4, then matrix AB has dimensions

    (A) 5×4
    (B) 5×5
    (C) 5×7
    (D) 7×4
    (E) 7×5

166

76. Let $x \therefore y$ be defined as the sum of all integers between x and y. For example, $1 \therefore 4 = 2 + 3 = 5$. What is the value of

$$(60 \therefore 900) - (63 \therefore 898) ?$$

(A) 1982
(B) 1983
(C) 1984
(D) 1985
(E) 1986

LEVEL 3: GEOMETRY

77. The set of points (a, b, c) such that

$$(a - 3)^2 + (b - 2)^2 + (c + 1)^2 = -1$$

is

(A) a sphere
(B) a circle
(C) a parabola
(D) a point
(E) empty

78. What is the x-coordinate of the vertex of the parabola whose equation is $y = x^2 - 6x + 3$?

(A) 0
(B) 1
(C) 2
(D) 3
(E) 4

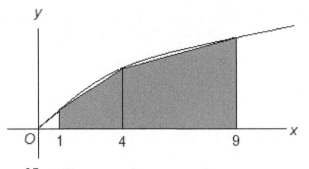

Note: Figure not drawn to scale.

79. The figure above shows a portion of the graph of $y = \sqrt{x}$. What is the sum of the areas of the two inscribed trapezoids shown?

    (A) 11
    (B) 17
    (C) 23
    (D) 34
    (E) 38

80. The hyperbola with equation $x^2 - (y - 2)^2 = 5$ crosses the x-axis when $x =$

    (A) 0 only
    (B) 3 only
    (C) 3 and -3 only
    (D) 0 and 3 only
    (E) 0, 3 and -3

81. A cone is inscribed in a cube of surface area 24 in such a way that its base touches four edges of the cube. What is the volume of the space enclosed by the cube, but NOT by the cone?

    (A) 1.6
    (B) 2.1
    (C) 4.0
    (D) 5.9
    (E) 7.3

82. A line has parametric equations $x = 1 - 7t$ and $y = -2 - 3t$, where t is the parameter. The slope of the line is

    (A) -2

    (B) $-\frac{1}{2}$

    (C) $\frac{3}{7}$

    (D) $\frac{7}{3}$

    (E) $\frac{7+2t}{3-t}$

83. A right circular cylinder has a base radius of 5 and a height of 4. If P and Q are two points on the surface of the cylinder, what is the maximum distance between P and Q?

    (A) 4.79
    (B) 6.40
    (C) 10.77
    (D) 10.92
    (E) 11.45

84. A sphere with a radius of 10 is centered at the origin. Which of the following points is NOT inside the sphere?

    (A) $(-5,5,-5)$
    (B) $(4, -5,6)$
    (C) $(1,7, -7)$
    (D) $(-4,-4,8)$
    (E) $(1,-8, -6)$

LEVEL 3: PROBABILITY AND STATISTICS

85. Of the following lists of numbers, which has the smallest standard deviation?

    (A) 6, 7, 8, 9, 10
    (B) 7, 8, 9, 10, 11
    (C) 6, 8, 10, 12, 14
    (D) 10, 10, 10, 10, 10
    (E) 6, 7, 10, 12, 13

86. If a 3-digit positive integer is chosen at random, what is the probability that an integer is chosen that contains only nonzero digits?

    (A) 0.99
    (B) 0.81
    (C) 0.64
    (D) 0.50
    (E) 0.01

87. 30 people are asked how many siblings they have. 2 of them have no siblings, 5 have 1 sibling, 12 have 2 siblings, 6 have 3 siblings, and 5 have 4 siblings. If one of these people were chosen at random, what is the probability that this person has 2 or more siblings?

    (A) 0.43
    (B) 0.70
    (C) 0.77
    (D) 0.84
    (E) 0.90

88. At a gathering, each of the seven people in attendance shakes hands with each of the other six people exactly three times. How many handshakes take place?

    (A) 21
    (B) 36
    (C) 42
    (D) 63
    (E) 126

LEVEL 3: TRIGONOMETRY

89. For $0 < x < \frac{\pi}{2}$,

    $$\cot x - \cot(-x) + \sec x - \sec(-x) + \csc x - \csc(-x) =$$

    (A) 0
    (B) 3
    (C) $2 \cot x$
    (D) $2 \cot x + 2 \csc x$
    (E) $2 \cot x + 2 \csc x + 2 \sec x$

90. If $\arccos(\cos x) = \dfrac{\pi}{6}$ and $0 < x < \pi$, then x could equal

    (A) 0

    (B) $\dfrac{\pi}{6}$

    (C) $\dfrac{\pi}{4}$

    (D) $\dfrac{\pi}{3}$

    (E) $\dfrac{\pi}{2}$

91. If $\sec x = 1.23$, then $\sec(\pi - x) =$

    (A) −1.23

    (B) −0.81

    (C) 0

    (D) 0.81

    (E) 1.23

92. The polar equation $r = 7$ defines a

    (A) point

    (B) circle

    (C) noncircular ellipse

    (D) line

    (E) limacon

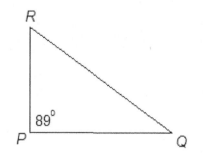

93. In the figure above, if $PR = 5$ and $PQ = 6$, then $RQ =$

    (A) 3.12

    (B) 3.33

    (C) 5.01

    (D) 6.23

    (E) 7.74

94. If $\cot x = k$, then for all x in the interval $0 < x < \frac{\pi}{2}$, $\sin x =$

   (A) $\dfrac{1}{1+k}$

   (B) $\dfrac{k}{\sqrt{1+k^2}}$

   (C) $\dfrac{1}{\sqrt{1+k^2}}$

   (D) $\dfrac{k}{\sqrt{1-k^2}}$

   (E) $\dfrac{1}{\sqrt{1-k^2}}$

95. $\cot(\sin^{-1} 0.23) =$

   (A) 0.23
   (B) 1.27
   (C) 2.11
   (D) 3.33
   (E) 4.23

96. $\sin x \sec x + \cos x \csc x =$

   (A) $\tan x \cos x$
   (B) $\tan x \sin x$
   (C) $\sin x \cos x$
   (D) $\sec x \csc x$
   (E) $\sec x \tan x$

LEVEL 4: NUMBER THEORY

97. If the magnitudes of vectors **u** and **v** are 3 and 11, respectively, then the magnitude of vector (**v** − **u**) CANNOT be

   (A) 8
   (B) 10
   (C) 12
   (D) 14
   (E) 16

172

98. If $k_0 = 1$ and $k_{n+1} = \frac{k_n}{\sqrt{3+k_n}}$, then $k_4 =$

    (A) 0.0833
    (B) 0.1479
    (C) 0.2673
    (D) 0.5
    (E) 1

99. If $i^2 = -1$, then $\frac{(3+5i)(3-5i)}{17} + i^{86} =$

    (A) -3
    (B) -2
    (C) -1
    (D) 0
    (E) 1

100. A statue weighing 1000 pounds loses 3% of its weight each year due to erosion. What is the weight of the statue in pounds after 15 years?

    (A) 372.6
    (B) 525.1
    (C) 633.3
    (D) 866.6
    (E) 899.5

LEVEL 4: ALGEBRA AND FUNCTIONS

101. If $k(x) = \log_5 \sqrt[3]{2x + 1}$, what is $k^{-1}(\frac{2}{3})$?

    (A) 8.7
    (B) 10.2
    (C) 11.5
    (D) 12.0
    (E) 13.2

102. If $x = 2i + 1$, then $x^2 - x + 4 =$

    (A) $2i$
    (B) i
    (C) 0
    (D) $-i$
    (E) $-2i$

$$x + y + z = 4$$
$$x - y = 2$$
$$2y + z = k$$

103. The system of equations above will have infinitely many real solutions when $k =$

   (A) -2
   (B) 0
   (C) 2
   (D) 4
   (E) 8

104. $\lim\limits_{x \to 3} \dfrac{x^3 + 2x^2 - 15x}{x - 3} =$

   (A) 3
   (B) 12
   (C) 24
   (D) $+\infty$
   (E) The limit does not exist

105. If $p(x)$ is a seventh degree polynomial, then which of the following could be the definition of $p(x)$?

   (A) $p(x) = (x - 1)(x - 4)(x - 2)$
   (B) $p(x) = x[(x - 1)^2]^2$
   (C) $p(x) = x^3(x - 1)^4$
   (D) $p(x) = x(x - 7)^2(x - 2)^5$
   (E) $p(x) = x^6(x - 1)^7$

106. The formula $A = P(1.025)^{2t}$ gives the amount A that an account will be worth after an initial investment P is compounded twice a year at an annual rate of 5% for t years. How many years will it take an initial investment to double?

   (A) 12.2
   (B) 14.0
   (C) 15.2
   (D) 17.6
   (E) 22.1

174

107. If $(2.47)^{2a}(2.47)^{3b} = (1.23)^{5b}$, what is the value of $\frac{a}{b}$?

    (A) −0.93
    (B) −0.75
    (C) −0.50
    (D) 0.27
    (E) 0.93

108. What is the remainder when $x^4 + 2x^3 - 7x + 2$ is divided by $x - 2$?

    (A) 2
    (B) 8
    (C) 12
    (D) 16
    (E) 20

LEVEL 4: GEOMETRY

109. What is the length of the minor axis of the ellipse whose equation is $50x^2 + 40y^2 = 180$?

    (A) 2.12
    (B) 3.79
    (C) 7.2
    (D) 8.49
    (E) 9

110. Which of the following is an equation for a square with sides of length 7?

    (A) $|x| + |y| = 7$

    (B) $|x| + |y| = \frac{7}{\sqrt{2}}$

    (C) $|x| - |y| = 7$

    (D) $|x||y| = \frac{7}{\sqrt{2}}$

    (E) $x^2 + y^2 = \frac{7}{2}$

111. Circles *A* and *B* are externally tangent circles, both with a radius of 3. If the center of circle *A* is $(-2,3)$, which of the following CANNOT be the center of circle *B* ?

   (A) $(-2, 9)$
   (B) $(-2,-3)$
   (C) $(-8, 3)$
   (D) $(1, 5)$
   (E) $(4, 3)$

112. If the complex number *z* is plotted as a point in the complex plane, it appears in the second quadrant. In which quadrant does $i(z + 2)$ lie?

   (A) I
   (B) II
   (C) III
   (D) IV
   (E) Cannot be determined from the given information

113. A sphere with volume 64 cubic inches is inscribed in a cube. What is the length of the long diagonal of the cube?

   (A) 7.6
   (B) 8.1
   (C) 8.6
   (D) 9.4
   (E) 9.9

114. Which of the following is the graph of a function that is both even and odd?

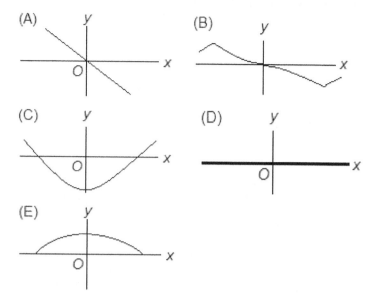

(A)

(B)

(C)

(D)

(E)

115. A square with vertices (1,0), (0,1), (−1,0), (0,−1) is rotated around the x-axis to generate a solid. What is the volume of this solid?

 (A) 1.05
 (B) 2.09
 (C) 3.24
 (D) 4.18
 (E) 5.00

116. Which of the following is an equation for the circle with radius 2 and center (1,−4) ?

 (A) $x^2 + y^2 - 2x + 8y + 13 = 0$
 (B) $x^2 + y^2 + 2x - 8y + 13 = 0$
 (C) $x^2 + y^2 - 2x + 8y + 11 = 0$
 (D) $x^2 + y^2 + 2x - 8y + 11 = 0$
 (E) $x^2 + y^2 - 2x + 8y - 4 = 0$

LEVEL 4: PROBABILITY AND STATISTICS

117. A five-digit number is randomly generated using each of the digits 1, 2, 3, 4, and 5 exactly once. What is the probability that the digits 2 and 3 are not next to each other?

    (A) 0.2
    (B) 0.3
    (C) 0.4
    (D) 0.5
    (E) 0.6

118. A pile of books consists of 3 red books, 7 yellow books, and 5 blue books. If 2 books are selected at random from the pile, what is the probability that neither book is yellow?

    (A) 0.73
    (B) 0.61
    (C) 0.50
    (D) 0.33
    (E) 0.27

Advertising expenditure (in thousands of dollars)	Monthly book sales (in thousands)
0	1
3	2
5	6
9	14

119. A publisher is investigating the relationship between advertising expenditures and monthly book sales. The data above represents this relationship for a small sample. If a least-squares exponential regression is used to model this data, what sales would be reported if 15 thousand dollars is spent on advertising?

    (A) 62,000
    (B) 67,000
    (C) 76,000
    (D) 82,000
    (E) 95,000

120. A group of students take a test and the average score is 90. One more student takes the test and receives a score of 81 decreasing the average score of the group to 87. How many students were in the initial group?

(A) 2
(B) 3
(C) 4
(D) 5
(E) 6

LEVEL 4: TRIGONOMETRY

121. If $90° < \theta < 180°$ and $\csc \theta = 7$, then $\sec \theta =$

(A) 1.01
(B) 1
(C) 0.99
(D) −1
(E) −1.01

122. What is the period of the graph of $= -4\sec(\frac{3}{7}\pi\theta - 1)$?

(A) $\frac{\pi}{3}$

(B) $\frac{7}{3}$

(C) $\frac{14}{3}$

(D) $\frac{14\pi}{3}$

(E) $\frac{14\pi}{15}$

123. Points P and Q lie on a circle of radius 12 with center O. If the measure of $\angle OPQ$ is 30°, what is the length of chord $\overline{PQ}$?

(A) 20.0
(B) 20.2
(C) 20.4
(D) 20.6
(E) 20.8

179

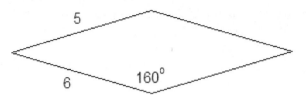

124. What is the area of the parallelogram shown in the figure above?

    (A) 9.23
    (B) 9.42
    (C) 9.55
    (D) 10.02
    (E) 10.26

125. A 7-foot ladder is leaning against a wall such that the angle relative to the level ground is 70°. Which of the following expressions involving cosine gives the distance, in feet, from the base of the ladder to the wall?

    (A) $\dfrac{7}{\cos 70°}$

    (B) $\dfrac{\cos 70°}{7}$

    (C) $\dfrac{1}{7\cos 70°}$

    (D) $7\cos 70°$

    (E) $\cos(7 \cdot 70°)$

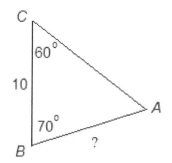

126. In $\triangle ABC$ shown above, the measure of $\angle B$ is 70°, the measure of $\angle C$ is 60°, and $\overline{BC}$ is 10 inches long. Which of the following is an expression for the length, in inches of $\overline{AB}$?

    (A) $\dfrac{10 \sin 50°}{\sin 70°}$

    (B) $\dfrac{10 \sin 60°}{\sin 50°}$

    (C) $\dfrac{10 \sin 130°}{\sin 70°}$

    (D) $\dfrac{10 \sin 70°}{\sin 50°}$

    (E) $\dfrac{10 \sin 60°}{\sin 70°}$

127. The vertex of $\angle P$ is the origin of the standard (x, y) coordinate plane. One ray of $\angle P$ is the positive x-axis. The other ray, $\overrightarrow{PQ}$, is positioned so that $\cos A < 0$ and $\tan A > 0$. In which quadrant, if it can be determined, is point Q ?

    (A) Quadrant I
    (B) Quadrant II
    (C) Quadrant III
    (D) Quadrant IV
    (E) Cannot be determined from the given information

128. For $0 < x < \dfrac{\pi}{2}$, the expression $\dfrac{\cos x}{\sqrt{1-\cos^2 x}} - \dfrac{\sqrt{1-\sin^2 x}}{\sin x}$ is equivalent to

    (A) 0
    (B) $\cot x$
    (C) $\tan x - 1$
    (D) $1 - \tan x$
    (E) $1 - \cot x$

LEVEL 5: NUMBER THEORY

129. Which of the following does <u>not</u> have an element that is greater than any other element in that set?

    I. The set of positive rational numbers q such that $q < 2$
    II. The set of positive rational numbers q such that $q^2 < 2$
    III. The set of positive rational numbers q such that $q^2 \leq 2$

    (A) None
    (B) I only
    (C) II only
    (D) III only
    (E) I, II, and III

130. The integer n is equal to k^3 for some integer k. Suppose that n is divisible by 45 and 400. The smallest possible value of n has the form ABC, DEF where $A, B, C, D, E,$ and F are digits. What is the product of A and C?

    (A) 12
    (B) 9
    (C) 6
    (D) 3
    (E) 2

131. $\sum_{k=1}^{100} 3k - 5 =$

    (A) 295
    (B) 7,575
    (C) 10,005
    (D) 14,650
    (E) 30,300

132. If $a > 0$ and $b > 1$, and $\log_b a^2 = 4k$, then which of the following can be FALSE?

    (A) $\log_b a = 2k$

    (B) $\log_{b^2} a = k$

    (C) $\log_{b^k} a = 2$

    (D) $\log_{b^k} \dfrac{a}{2} = 1$

    (E) $\log_{b^{4k}} a = \dfrac{1}{2}$

LEVEL 5: ALGEBRA AND FUNCTIONS

$$x + 2y + z = 3$$
$$2y + 3z = 2$$
$$x + 7z = 9$$

133. If we rewrite the system of equations above in the matrix form $AX = B$, then what is $|A|$?

   (A) 20
   (B) 18
   (C) 16
   (D) 15
   (E) 12

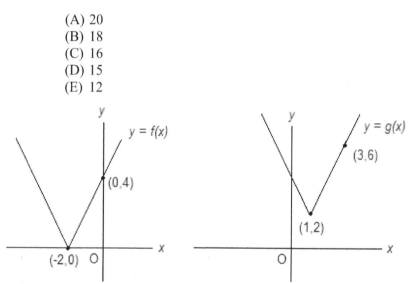

134. The figures above show the graphs of the functions f and g. The function f is defined by $f(x) = 2|x + 2|$ and the function g is defined by $g(x) = f(x + h) + k$, where h and k are constants. What is the value of $|h - k|$?

   (A) 1
   (B) 2
   (C) 3
   (D) 4
   (E) 5

135. Consider the functions $f(x) = \sqrt{x-1}$ and $g(x) = ax + b$. In the standard (x, y) coordinate plane, $y = f(g(x))$ passes through $(0, 1)$ and $(2, 3)$. What is the value of $a + b$?

   (A) 1
   (B) 2
   (C) 4
   (D) 5
   (E) 6

136. For all x in the domain of the function $\frac{x+2}{x^3-x}$, this function is equivalent to:

   (A) $\frac{1}{x^2-1} + \frac{2}{x^3-x}$

   (B) $\frac{2}{x^2-1}$

   (C) $\frac{1}{x^2-1}$

   (D) $\frac{1}{x-1}$

   (E) $\frac{1}{x+1}$

137. The system of equations

$$x + y + z = 1$$
$$x + z = 3$$
$$y + bz = c$$

has infinitely many solutions when

   (A) $b = c = 0$
   (B) $b = c = 1$
   (C) $b = c = -2$
   (D) $b = 0$ and $c = 2$
   (E) $b = 0$ and $c = -2$

138. If $f(x) = g(x) - h(x)$, where $g(x) = 8x^2 + 13x - 17$ and $h(x) = 8x^2 - 9x + 16$, then $f(x)$ is <u>always</u> divisible by which of the following?

   (A) 5
   (B) 7
   (C) 9
   (D) 11
   (E) 13

184

139. $\lim\limits_{x \to \infty} \frac{\sqrt{3x^2 - 1}}{2x - 5} =$

    (A) $\frac{1}{2}$

    (B) $\frac{\sqrt{3}}{2}$

    (C) $\frac{3}{2}$

    (D) ∞

    (E) The limit does not exist

140. If $g(x, y) = xy$ for all real numbers x and y, $g(j, k) = 10$, $g(k, m) = 35$, and $g(j, m) = 56$, which of the following could be the value of jkm ?

    (A) 70
    (B) 100
    (C) 140
    (D) 280
    (E) 360

LEVEL 5: GEOMETRY

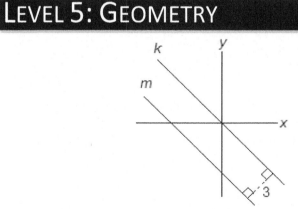

141. In the figure above, line k has the equation $y = -x$. Line m is below line k, as shown, and m is parallel to k. Which of the following is an equation for line m ?

    (A) $y = -x + 3$
    (B) $y = -x + \sqrt{3}$
    (C) $y = -x - 3\sqrt{2}$
    (D) $y = -3x$
    (E) $y = -3x + 3$

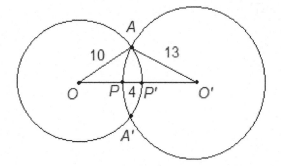

142. The circles above, centered at O and O' intersect at A and A', and points O, P, P', and O' are collinear. $OA = 10$, $O'A = 13$, and $PP' = 4$. What is the length of OO' ?

    (A) 19
    (B) 20
    (C) 21
    (D) 22
    (E) 23

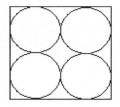

143. In the figure above, all 4 circles are congruent and each circle is tangent to each circle adjacent to it, and two sides of the square. The area of each circle is 2π inches. What is the length, in inches, of each side of the square?

    (A) $\sqrt{2}$
    (B) 2
    (C) $2\sqrt{2}$
    (D) 4
    (E) $4\sqrt{2}$

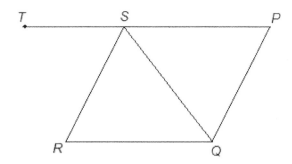

144. In the figure above, $\overline{QS}$ is the shorter diagonal of rhombus $PQRS$ and T is on $\overleftrightarrow{PS}$. The measure of angle PQS is $x°$. What is the measure of RST, in terms of x ?

(A) $x°$

(B) $2x°$

(C) $\frac{1}{2}x°$

(D) $90° - x°$

(E) $180° - 2x°$

145. A triangle is formed by the x-axis, the y-axis, and the line $y = c^2x + c$, where c is a positive real number. What is the volume of the cone generated by rotating this triangle around the y-axis?

(A) $\frac{\pi}{3}$

(B) $\frac{c\pi}{3}$

(C) $\frac{\pi}{3c}$

(D) $\frac{3}{\pi}$

(E) $\frac{3c}{\pi}$

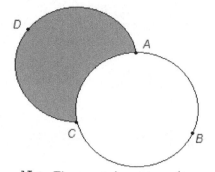

Note: Figure not drawn to scale.

146. In the above figure, arcs *ABC* and *ADC* each measure 270 degrees and each of these arcs is part of a circle of radius 8 inches. What is the area of the shaded region to the nearest inch?

    (A) 165
    (B) 166
    (C) 167
    (D) 168
    (E) 169

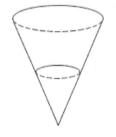

147. The right circular cone pictured above is cut horizontally at the midpoint of its height. If the smaller piece has a height of 3 and a volume of 9π, what is the volume of the larger piece?

    (A) 12π
    (B) 21π
    (C) 63π
    (D) 216π
    (E) 284π

148. A square is inscribed in a circle of diameter d. What is the perpendicular distance from the center of the circle to a side of the square, in terms of d?

(A) $\frac{d}{2}$

(B) $\frac{d\sqrt{2}}{4}$

(C) $\frac{d\sqrt{2}}{2}$

(D) d

(E) $d\sqrt{2}$

LEVEL 5: PROBABILITY AND STATISTICS

149. Suppose that the average (arithmetic mean) of a, b, and c is h, the average of b, c, and d is j, the average of c, d, and e is k, and the average of d, e, and f is m. What is the value of $(a + c) - (d + f)$?

(A) $h - j + k - m$

(B) $3(h - j + k - m)$

(C) $\frac{3}{4}(h - j + k - m)$

(D) $3(h + j + k + m)$

(E) $\frac{3}{4}(h + j + k - m)$

150. How many ways are there to line up 4 men and 3 women if two people of the same gender are not allowed to stand next to each other?

(A) 6

(B) 24

(C) 36

(D) 72

(E) 144

151. If 2 real numbers between 0 and 10 are randomly chosen, what is the probability that the distance between them is at most 7?

    (A) 0.91
    (B) 0.87
    (C) 0.85
    (D) 0.79
    (E) 0.70

152. A positive integer is called a palindrome if it reads the same forward as it does backward. For example, 1661 is a palindrome. If n is a positive integer, how many palindromes are there of length $2n$?

    (A) n
    (B) 10^{n-1}
    (C) 10^n
    (D) $9 \cdot 10^{n-1}$
    (E) $9 \cdot 10^n$

LEVEL 5: TRIGONOMETRY

153. A ladder rests against the side of a wall and reaches a point that is h meters above the ground. The angle formed by the ladder and the ground is $\theta°$. A point on the ladder is k meters from the wall. What is the vertical distance, in meters, from this point on the ladder to the ground?

    (A) $(h - k) \tan \theta°$
    (B) $(h - k) \cos \theta°$
    (C) $h - k \sin \theta°$
    (D) $h - k \cos \theta°$
    (E) $h - k \tan \theta°$

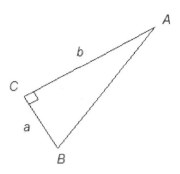

154. In the right triangle above, $b > a > 0$. One of the angle measures in the triangle is $\sin^{-1} \frac{b}{\sqrt{a^2+b^2}}$. What is $\tan[\sin^{(-1)}\left(\frac{b}{\sqrt{a^2+b^2}}\right)]$?

    (A) $\frac{b}{a}$

    (B) $\frac{a}{b}$

    (C) $\frac{b}{\sqrt{a^2+b^2}}$

    (D) $\frac{a}{\sqrt{a^2+b^2}}$

    (E) $\frac{\sqrt{a^2+b^2}}{a}$

155. If $\arccos(\cos x) = \frac{\pi}{4}$ and $0 \le x \le 2\pi$, then x could equal

    (A) 0

    (B) $\frac{\pi}{6}$

    (C) $\frac{\pi}{3}$

    (D) $\frac{3\pi}{4}$

    (E) $\frac{7\pi}{4}$

156. If $0 < x < \frac{\pi}{2}$, then $\sec(\arctan x) =$

   (A) $\frac{1}{x}$

   (B) $\frac{1}{\sqrt{x^2+1}}$

   (C) $\sqrt{x^2 + 1}$

   (D) $\frac{1}{\sqrt{1-x^2}}$

   (E) $\sqrt{1 - x^2}$

LEVEL 6 PROBLEMS

157. A ball is dropped from a height of 20 feet above the ground, and after each bounce it rebounds to one fourth of its previous height. What is the total distance, in feet, travelled by the ball?

   (A) 6.67
   (B) 26.66
   (C) 33.33
   (D) 66.67
   (E) 80.00

158. $\lim\limits_{x \to -\infty} \dfrac{\sqrt{7x^6+3x^8}}{6-5x^2+2x^4} =$

   (A) $\frac{-\sqrt{7}}{2}$

   (B) $\frac{-\sqrt{3}}{2}$

   (C) $\frac{\sqrt{7}}{6}$

   (D) $\frac{\sqrt{3}}{2}$

   (E) $-\infty$

192

159. Let k be the smallest positive integer such that $\frac{k}{2}$ is a perfect square and $\frac{k}{3}$ is a perfect cube. Then the prime factorization of k has the form $2^c 3^d$ for positive integers c and d. What is the smallest positive integer divisible by both c and d?

    (A) 1
    (B) 3
    (C) 4
    (D) 6
    (E) 12

160. Let j and k be positive integers with $j \leq k$. In how many ways can k be written as a sum of j positive integers? (For example, if $j = 2$ and $k = 3$, then we can write $k = 1 + 2 = 2 + 1$. So, in this case the answer is 2).

    (A) $_{k-1}C_{j-1}$

    (B) $_{k-1}P_{j-1}$

    (C) $_k C_j$

    (D) $_k P_j$

    (E) $\frac{k!}{j!}$

ANSWERS TO
SUPPLEMENTAL PROBLEMS

LEVEL 1: NUMBER THEORY

1. C
2. B
3. E
4. E

LEVEL 1: ALGEBRA AND FUNCTIONS

5. C
6. D
7. C
8. A
9. D
10. C
11. C
12. D

LEVEL 1: GEOMETRY

13. C
14. E
15. E
16. C
17. E
18. B
19. D
20. B

194

LEVEL 1: PROBABILITY AND STATISTICS

21. B
22. C
23. A
24. D

LEVEL 1: TRIGONOMETRY

25. E
26. E
27. A
28. B
29. E
30. B
31. C
32. E

LEVEL 2: NUMBER THEORY

33. E
34. D
35. E
36. E

LEVEL 2: ALGEBRA AND FUNCTIONS

37. E
38. C
39. D
40. A
41. E
42. D
43. A
44. C

LEVEL 2: GEOMETRY

45. C
46. B
47. A
48. A
49. B
50. B
51. E
52. B

LEVEL 2: PROBABILITY AND STATISTICS

53. B
54. A
55. D
56. C

LEVEL 2: TRIGONOMETRY

57. A
58. D
59. E
60. E
61. D
62. A
63. E
64. C

LEVEL 3: NUMBER THEORY

65. C
66. A
67. B
68. D

LEVEL 3: ALGEBRA AND FUNCTIONS

69. C
70. E
71. C
72. C
73. C
74. C
75. A
76. B

LEVEL 3: GEOMETRY

77. E
78. D
79. B
80. C
81. D
82. C
83. C
84. E

LEVEL 3: PROBABILITY AND STATISTICS

85. D
86. B
87. C
88. D

LEVEL 3: TRIGONOMETRY

89. D
90. B
91. A
92. B
93. E
94. C
95. E
96. D

LEVEL 4: NUMBER THEORY

97. E
98. A
99. E
100. C

LEVEL 4: ALGEBRA AND FUNCTIONS

101. D
102. A
103. C
104. C
105. C
106. B
107. A
108. E

LEVEL 4: GEOMETRY

109. B
110. B
111. D
112. E
113. C
114. D
115. B
116. A

LEVEL 4: PROBABILITY AND STATISTICS

117. E
118. E
119. E
120. A

LEVEL 4: TRIGONOMETRY

121. E
122. C
123. E
124. E
125. D
126. B
127. C
128. A

LEVEL 5: NUMBER THEORY

129. E
130. A
131. D
132. D

LEVEL 5: ALGEBRA AND FUNCTIONS

133. B
134. E
135. E
136. A
137. E
138. D
139. B
140. C

LEVEL 5: GEOMETRY

141. C
142. A
143. E
144. E
145. C
146. A
147. C
148. B

LEVEL 5: PROBABILITY AND STATISTICS

149. B
150. E
151. A
152. D

LEVEL 5: TRIGONOMETRY

153. E
154. A
155. E
156. C

LEVEL 6 PROBLEMS

157. C
158. D
159. E
160. A

YOUR ROAD
TO SUCCESS

Congratulations! By practicing the problems in this book you have given yourself a significant boost to your SAT Math Level 2 Subject Test score. Go ahead and take a practice test. The math score you get should be much higher than the score you received on your last practice test.

What should you do to get your score even higher? Good news! You can use this book over and over again to continue to increase your score – right up to an 800. All you need to do is change the problems you are focusing on.

For each of the five subject areas go back and focus on problems that are right at and slightly above your current ability level. For example, if you have gotten all the Level 2 Geometry questions right, but you are still getting a few Level 3 Geometry questions wrong, then focus on Level 3 and 4 Geometry problems. Do this independently for each subject area.

Upon your next reading, try to solve each problem that you attempt in up to four different ways

- Using an SAT specific math strategy.
- The quickest way you can think of.
- The way you would do it in school.
- The easiest way for you.

Remember – the actual answer is not very important. What is important is to learn as many techniques as possible. This is the best way to simultaneously increase your current score, and increase your level of mathematical maturity. Keep doing problems from this book for about twenty minutes each day right up until two days before the test. Mark off the ones you get wrong and attempt them over and over again each week until you can get them right on your own.

I really want to thank you for putting your trust in me and my materials, and I want to assure you that you have made excellent use of your time by studying with this book. I wish you the best of luck on the SAT Math Subject Test, on getting into your choice college, and in life.

Dr. Steve Warner
steve@SATPrepGet800.com

ACTIONS TO COMPLETE AFTER YOU HAVE READ THIS BOOK

1. Take another practice test

You should see a substantial improvement in your score.

2. Continue to practice SAT math subject test problems for 10 to 20 minutes each day

Keep practicing problems of the appropriate levels until two days before the test.

3. Use my Facebook page for additional help

If you feel you need extra help that you cannot get from this book, please feel free to post your questions on my Facebook wall at www.facebook.com/SATPrepGet800.

4. Review this book

If this book helped you, please post your positive feedback on the site you purchased it from; e.g. Amazon, Barnes and Noble, etc.

5. Visit my website www.SATPrepGet800.com

You will find free content here that is updated weekly to help with your SAT preparation.

6. Follow me on twitter

www.twitter.com/SATPrepGet800

About the Author

Dr. Steve Warner, a New York native, earned his Ph.D. at Rutgers University in Pure Mathematics in May, 2001. While a graduate student,

Dr. Warner won the TA Teaching Excellence Award.

After Rutgers, Dr. Warner joined the Penn State Mathematics Department as an Assistant Professor. In September, 2002, Dr. Warner returned to New York to accept an Assistant Professor position at Hofstra University. By September 2007, Dr. Warner had received tenure and was promoted to Associate Professor. He has taught undergraduate and graduate courses in Precalculus, Calculus, Linear Algebra, Differential Equations, Mathematical Logic, Set Theory and Abstract Algebra.

Over that time, Dr. Warner participated in a five year NSF grant, "The MSTP Project," to study and improve mathematics and science curriculum in poorly performing junior high schools. He also published several articles in scholarly journals, specifically on Mathematical Logic.

Dr. Warner has more than 15 years of experience in general math tutoring and tutoring for standardized tests such as the SAT, ACT and AP Calculus exams. He has tutored students both individually and in group settings.

In February, 2010 Dr. Warner released his first SAT prep book "The 32 Most Effective SAT Math Strategies," and in 2012 founded Get 800 Test Prep. Since then Dr. Warner has written books for the SAT, ACT, GRE, SAT Math Subject Tests and AP Calculus exams.

Dr. Steve Warner can be reached at

steve@SATPrepGet800.com

BOOKS BY DR. STEVE WARNER

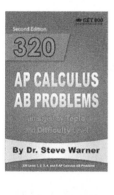